# CASE STUDIES IN FAMILY THERAPY
## *An Integrative Approach*

WILLIAM M. WALSH, Ph.D.
University of Northern Colorado

**ALLYN AND BACON**
*Boston   London   Toronto   Sydney   Tokyo   Singapore*

Managing Editor: Susan Badger
Series Editorial Assistant: Dana Lamothe
Production Coordinator: Lisa Feder
Editorial-Production Service: York Production Services
Cover Administrator: Linda Dickinson
Cover Designer: Suzanne Harbison
Manufacturing Buyer: Megan Cochran

Copyright © 1991 by Allyn and Bacon
A Division of Simon & Schuster, Inc.
160 Gould Street
Needham Heights, Massachusetts 02194

Walsh, William M.
    Case studies in family therapy : an integrative approach /
William M. Walsh.
        p.  cm.
    ISBN 0-205-12828-9
    1. Family psychotherapy—Case studies.  I. Title.
    [DNLM: 1. Family Therapy—case studies.  WM 430.5.F2 W228c]
RC488.5.W347  1991
616.89'158—dc20
DNLM/DLC
For Library of Congress                                    90-1165
                                                              CIP

Printed in the United States of America

10  9  8  7  6  5  4  3  2  1    95  94  93  92  91  90

Without a family, man, alone in the world,
trembles in the cold.
Andre Maurois

Happiness is having a large, loving, caring,
close-knit family in another city.
George Burns

# Contents

v

# Introduction

As the field of family therapy has evolved from its most famous beginnings in the work of both Murray Bowen and the Palo Alto Group, it has developed and expanded in an attempt to discover new ways of describing and treating human problems. The first seminal theories were developed by pioneer thinkers working on the theoretical edge of the helping professions. At first not widely accepted, their work has now become mainstream in the literature of the helping professions. These early thinkers are often referred to as the first generation of family therapy theorists. Their ranks are peopled by the likes of Gregory Bateson, Donald Jackson, Jay Haley, Virginia Satir, Murray Bowen, and Gerald Patterson. Today, their ideas and techniques are widely used in therapy and research. However, new models have appeared on the scene to rival the effectiveness of the original theories. Some of these models are modifications of the seminal theories, while others are a blending of their most popular concepts. These modified or blended models are often referred to as second generation models. Articles relating to their continued development and refinement now pepper the professional literature. The remainder of this book is devoted to one of these blended models.

Integrative Family Therapy is a second-generation theoretical model of family therapy. It is a blending of several major interpersonal models with an intrapsychic component. The theory of therapy is described in Part I, and includes a theory of personality for family assessment and a counseling process for treatment. This theory provides the basis for the ten cases that are presented in the remaining sections of the book.

Each case is presented in a standardized format. The intent is to present Integrative Family Therapy as a working model in full-length treatment processes. The cases can be approached in three ways. One way is to read each case for its informational value, or, in other words, how people enter, proceed through, and terminate therapy. This might be considered a more recreational or superficial approach to the material. A second way is to look at each case as through the eyes of a particular school of therapy, and to use the case material as data to test the efficacy of that particular model. The third method is to apply the principles of the Integrative Model as both assessment and treatment, and then to see how the case was actually treated in practice. This last approach is the primary intention of the author and is the reason that the text is organized in a standardized manner. When using Integrative Family Therapy, the counselor proceeds in the structured fashion presented in each case. From the initial phone contact to the final follow-up phone interview, the therapist moves from one stage of therapy to another in a relatively prescribed fashion. The theory and process are described in Part I. Parts II through IV demonstrate its application with families.

Each case is divided into eleven sections. The first three sections provide all of the information that is used for the family assessment. Section I, Identifying Data, consists of the basic information such as names, ages, schools attended, and the like. It is the type of information that a therapist receives from a data intake sheet or from several questions during the initial phone call. Section II, Introductory Material, is essentially a statement of the presenting problem or the reason for the referral. Section III is a description of the first two therapy sessions. In most cases, the material is presented in the same order as it occurred in the sessions. The intention is that the reader will get the feeling of being in the therapy room and receiving the data as it is occurring. Occasionally, conversations are summarized for brevity. The material is not presented as a case transcript but rather as a detailed summary of the personal interactions. All of the material presented in these three sections is later organized on an assessment sheet for the complete assessment of the family.

Part IV is a blank evaluation sheet. This is similar to the sheet that the Integrative Family Therapist uses to organize the data that has been culled from the initial contacts and the first two sessions. Generally, two sessions are sufficient to gather the essential data. The reader may fill out the evaluation sheet based on an understanding of the model and the information that has been presented thus far. It is the same material that the therapists used in the assessment of the case. A blank assessment card is presented in Section V. This is to be completed by the reader using the information that was organized on the evaluation sheet. Again, this is the process used by the therapist who treated the case.

Sections VI and VII contain the completed evaluation sheet and assessment card that were prepared by the therapists prior to the third session. This is an opportunity for the readers to check their own work against the Integrative Family Therapists' conclusions and to plan the future sessions in the counseling process. Session three, the feedback session, is described in Section VIII. Section IX contains a discussion of all other sessions, and gives the reader the opportunity to observe the interventions by the therapists and the changes that resulted in the families. Readers can decide how they would have treated each case and can speculate on the effectiveness of their own ideas for that particular situation. Section X describes the termination and follow-up phase, and Section XI contains the reactions and evaluation of the therapists and their supervisors. Hopefully, the evaluations are objective and accurate. Some admittedly are anguished, and others express the joy of assisting people to grow and problem-solve. Each process is rated on a goal attainment scale by the therapy supervisors. The scale is not a measurement instrument but rather a visual representation on a brief continuum of the achievement of the goals presented on the assessment card. The reader is invited to rate the therapeutic process also.

## *Goal Attainment Scale*

| 1 | 2 | 3 | 4 | 5 |
|---|---|---|---|---|
| no goals attained 0% | few goals attained 25% | half of goals attained 50% | most goals attained 75% | all goals attained 100% |

The cases are all taken from a university-based metropolitan treatment clinic that served a community consisting of varied ethnic, racial, and socioeconomic groups. The families were referred by school counselors and community mental health workers to the training component of the clinic. As part of a postgraduate family therapy program, the counselors worked in pairs under supervision. All of the sessions were videotaped. They were also viewed by supervisors through a one-way mirror. The ten cases were selected to represent different family developmental levels, ethnic groups, socioeconomic strata, and presenting problems.

The cases are presented in three parts organized by the developmental level of the family. Part II focuses on two families that contain preadolescent children. The first is a stepfamily with three children, and case two involves a single parent with two boys. Part III addresses the needs and concerns of six families with adolescent children. They cover the spectrum of intact, single-parent, and stepfamilies, as well as a variety of presenting problems and family dynamics. Part IV contains two cases that deal with the problems of two families with adult children. Altogether, they represent a panorama of concerns that permeate our society, and demonstrate the often different styles of therapists working in the same theoretical model. All of the cases do not represent successful treatment outcomes. What they do show is the real-life struggle of people in pain and the attempts of professionals to alleviate the dysfunction in the systems.

## Acknowledgments

I would like to express my deep appreciation to the families, therapists, and supervisors who participated in the therapeutic project; to Marsha Goldberg, James Fruehling and Judith Praul for their friendship and academic support.

A special thank you goes to the authors and co-authors of the cases; to Molly Allen and Linda Smith for their constructive editing of the final manuscript.

As always, a loving thank you to my wife, Kathleen.

# SUBJECT AREA GRID:  A Guide to Using This Casebook

| TOPIC AREAS | \_CASES\_ | | | | | | | | | |
|---|---|---|---|---|---|---|---|---|---|---|
| | 1 | 2 | 3 | 4 | 5 | 6 | 7 | 8 | 9 | 10 |
| Adult Children | | | | X | | | | | X | X |
| Alcoholism | X | X | X | | | X | X | | X | |
| Blended Families | X | | | | X | X | | | X | |
| Co-dependency | X | X | | | | | | X | X | |
| Dating | | X | | | | | | | | |
| Divorce Conflicts | | X | | | X | | | X | | |
| Drug Abuse | | | | X | | | X | | X | |
| Extended Family | | | | | | | X | X | X | X |
| Family Violence | | | X | | | | | | | |
| Financial Stress | X | X | | | | | | | X | |
| Grief | | | | | | | | X | | X |
| Homosexuality | | | | | | | | | X | |
| Infidelity | | | X | | | | | | | |
| Irresponsibility | X | X | X | X | X | X | X | | X | |
| Legal Conflicts | | | | X | | | | X | | |
| Marital Break-up | | | X | | | | | | | |
| Marital Conflict | | | X | | | X | | | | |
| Mental Illness | | X | | | | | | | | |
| Non-custodial Parent | | X | | | X | | X | X | | |
| Parent/child Conflict | X | | X | X | X | X | X | X | X | X |
| Parental Conflict | X | | X | | X | X | | | X | X |
| Peer Relationships | | | | X | | | | X | | |
| Physical Abuse | | X | X | | | | | | | |
| School Problems | | | X | X | | X | X | X | X | X |
| Sexual Abuse | X | | | | | | | | | |
| Sibling Conflict | X | X | | | | X | X | | | |
| Single Parent | | X | | X | | | X | X | X | |
| Suicide | | | X | | X | | | | | X |
| Teenage Pregnancy | | | | X | | | | | | |
| Work/school Stress | X | | | | | | | | | |

# List of Contributors

Leah Bergen, ED.M., M.A., NBCC
Executive Director, National Foundation for Children's Sleep and Related Disorders
Counselor, Chicago Public Schools

Paul Farina, M.A.
Supervisor, Domestic Violence Program
Circuit Court of Cook County, Illinois

Janice McIntyre, M.A.
PhD Candidate, Mississippi State University
Psychotherapist, Crossroads Counseling Center
Arlington Heights, Illinois

Ronald Melman, M.A.
Counselor, Special Education
Chicago Public Schools

Thomas Reagan, M.ED.
Probation Officer
Cook County Juvenile Court, Chicago

Linda Smith, M.ED.
PSY.D. Candidate, University of Northern Colorado
Psychotherapist, Greeley, Colorado

Bernadette Veeneman, M.ED., M.A.
Instructor, Loyola University, Chicago
Psychotherapist, Evanston, Illinois

# PART I

# Integrative Family Therapy: Theory of Therapy

**Theory of Personality**
  Family Tasks
  Family Growth Process
  General Personality Concepts
  Specific Personality Concepts

**Therapeutic Process**
  Stages in Therapy

# THEORY OF PERSONALITY

Therapy begins with a search for the meaning of human behavior. The therapist asks: "Why is this individual (or family) experiencing enough anxiety or dysfunction to cause him or her (them) to seek help or to be compelled by others to ask for assistance?" All therapists who develop therapy models have beliefs or concepts that explain the human condition. Whether these are cognitive, affective, historical, or systems based on some combination of these, they all attempt to understand behavior so that appropriate interventions can be developed.

Most therapy models focus on abnormal, deviant, or dysfunctional behavior. The concepts of these theories are developed to describe and treat undesirable behavior. Little if any space is allotted for discussion of healthy functioning. Thus, this type of system is particularly well-suited for therapists who work primarily with clinical or psychiatric populations. These systems are less appropriate for those of us who work mainly with the less deviant "normal" range of problems. In fact, most nonpsychiatric outpatient therapy is conducted with clients whose functioning in society ranges from marginal to very good. This "normal" client population does not need periodic hospitalization. These clients do not need major personality change. Instead, they wish to change aspects of themselves that are limiting their functioning or making them unhappy. Since most marriage and family therapy fall into this category, it is helpful to begin by describing healthy functioning. Once the primary aspects of a well-functioning family are identified, deviations from that norm can be isolated and treated.

## Family Tasks

In order to be considered well-functioning, there are a number of tasks that a family must fulfill. The following is a list of those that Integrative Family Therapy (IFT) considers to be most critical for the healthy development of the family. The reader may wish to add more tasks, as appropriate.

1. Teaching.
2. Support.
3. Stability.
4. Mutuality/privacy.

5. Independence/dependence.
6. Defining expectations.
7. Problem solving.

One of the most important human tasks is teaching/learning. Traditionally, the family has been the major vehicle for communicating forms of knowledge and skills. The parents or grandparents are the first teachers a child encounters. The learning process begins in early infancy.

This may seem like a simple concept. However, in our society, we increasingly find that parents are doing less teaching. Instead, they are relying on other societal institutions to relay critical knowledge. When faced with the task of influencing their children, parents are often confused about what they should be saying or doing. Such parents are easily swayed by new trends or pseudo experts.

After the learning process has been (hopefully) established, the teaching/learning continues. As children mature in a healthy way, they teach their parents new ideas and new ways of behaving. In this manner, a growth-producing teaching/learning process develops among all family members. The openness and mutuality of this process can be a barometer of a family's health.

A second task of the family unit is to provide support for its individual members. Steady financial support is basic to the continuing growth of all members, but emotional support and encouragement are equally important. An absence of either can promote insecurity and can become a source of debilitating anxiety for adults and children.

A closely related yet separate task is that of the provision of stability in family relationships. Set patterns of behavior for all family members can give structure in a confusing and changeable world. Children like to know when their father or mother will be away or at home. Thus, regular routines for parents are a source of security for kids. A permanent living arrangement, set times for going to bed and rising, consistent mealtimes, and seasonal traditions are all ways of providing stability in families.

Two other closely related tasks are the promotion of mutuality/privacy and the development of independence. Mutuality refers to the process of a family's working together for common goals. Each member knows that he or she can depend on others for help in time of need. However, each member also needs private time and space to grow as an individual, apart from the family unit. In particular, adolescents need mutuality/privacy. But all family members need a place and time to call their own.

The encouragement of independence is crucial for the gradual development of a healthy self-concept for each family member. Children must be taught and encouraged to function on their own in some situations, dependent only on themselves. This process should begin in early childhood with age-appropriate behaviors. A child can be given increasingly difficult chores that must be completed alone. For example, a child of four might be expected to dress himself or herself every day. At six years, a child should be expected to take reasonable care of toys. By ten, a child could be expected to make a contribution to the care and maintenance of the home. Chores that are geared to the child's age can give the child a feeling of self-importance and self-worth. As the child matures, he or she should be given more responsibilities and decisions. This process results in the gradual development of independent behaviors and adultlike reactions. The overall goal is the development of an independently functioning person.

The sixth task, defining expectations, appears to be one of the most common problems in all families. Setting unrealistic expectations for individuals or for the family unit is often a source of conflict and unhappiness. However, the establishment of reasonable short- and long-term goals is essential for orderly development. The emphasis in this task is on "reasonable." What can people reasonably expect from themselves and from others on a daily and yearly basis? Is there a good chance that goals will be reached? In this context, "reasonable expectations" refer to those that are acceptable to all concerned. In addition, they must have a good chance of being accomplished. This is more likely to occur in a family atmosphere of open discussion and mutual decision-making. All family members should feel free to affirm or negate, accept or reject, and to establish or change personal and family expectations. This, of course, is a continuous process that requires considerable commitment from all family members involved.

The final task relates specifically to the problem-solving process, which is present in every family member and every family unit. The key question for this task is: "How are problems defined and resolved in the immediate present?" Is a rigid process used, which tolerates little or no new input? Or is a flexible process used, which seeks out new data in an attempt to find new solutions or alternatives? The way a family handles insignificant daily problems is a key to how its members attempt to deal with important conflicts. Flexibility and openness are the prime ingredients in a satisfying problem-solving process. Much of what happens in family therapy revolves around helping people to establish and maintain rewarding problem-solving approaches to living. The remainder of this section will be devoted to this topic.

*Family Growth Process*

At this point, it might be helpful to examine two issues: how problems develop in a family, and how they are handled in functional and dysfunctional ways. It is possible to identify a family growth process. The following chart and discussion display a conceptualization that tracks healthy and unhealthy directions that a family may choose as part of this growth process.

## Family Growth Process

A. Two individuals come together, forming a relationship. This relationship usually involves a marriage commitment. Each half of the couple brings to the new relationship his or her own background from family of origin and his or her own personality dynamics.

B. From the very beginning, the relationship develops its own dynamics and characteristics; the two people develop methods for dealing with one another in the intimate arrangement. They create joint ways of interacting with the outside world. Eventually, this couple may have children, broadening the number of possible interactions in the new family.

C. The family members' maturation and aging process produce conflict and strain. Stress is produced when, in the process of daily living, individual members interact among themselves and with the outside world. They attempt to cope with the stress and resolve conflicts on the basis of "A" (the unique relationship), "B" (the relationship's dynamics and characteristics), and new data from the outside world. All of these sources may be appropriate and functional, or they may be distorted and dysfunctional.

Families with functional problem solving—"D"—are less likely to be in therapy. Instead, they go directly to "I" and resolve future stress and conflict. Families without functional problem solving end up in dysfunction—"E"—and are more likely to be in therapy.

D. If the family has established a functional process (i.e., appropriate "A" and "B" relationship formation and development of unique dynamics and characteristics) and incorporates new data, it will achieve resolution by dealing with the stress and conflict. The family members are then free to continue with satisfying daily living. In IFT terminology, the successful family has a well-functioning problem-solving process. A remarriage family (which is rapidly becoming a common family type) is particularly vulnerable at this stage. For remarriage families, both "A" and "B" involve very complex dynamics, and more people than the traditional family. In addition, there is the well-documented (Walsh 1989) aspect of the "instant family." Thus, for a reconstituted family, "E" (dysfunction) is more likely than than "D" (functional processes).

E. Dysfunction results when a family does not have a healthy problem-solving process. The immediate stress or conflict is not resolved, leaving unfinished feelings to linger. The result is interrupted daily living.

F. Frequently, families perpetuate the dysfunction by refusing to change (rigid problem solving) or by not being knowledgeable about the alternatives available to them.

G. Dysfunction is eventually expressed in one or more of the individuals in the family. When the unhealthy process has occurred for years, the family is no longer capable of containing the stress and pressure. It is at this point that a professional could enter the picture. The family may seek help on its own. Remarriage families tend to do this earlier than do traditional families. This is possibly due to a greater sensitivity on the part of remarriage families to potential difficulties.

It is more likely, however, that another societal institution will refer the family for treatment after noticing the family's difficulties. Educational institutions or law enforcement agencies are frequently the first to notice disruption in either a family unit or an individual member. Hence, these two particular institutions are prime referral agents for therapy. The family may refuse to recognize the problem or seek professional help. In this instance, it is likely that the family's problems will con-

tinue. It is possible that the problems will intensify. Spontaneous recovery is unlikely.

**H.** If the family chooses to seek professional help, the therapeutic
intervention process begins. Ideally, a professional begins by
identifying the dysfunction, then helps the family to make re-
mediative changes. The process may be short- or long-term.
Hopefully, the family members develop new ways of relating
to one another, new problem-solving methods, and a greater
understanding of themselves and others.

**I.** After termination of therapy, the family can meet and resolve
future stress and conflict.

This discussion of the nature of the family growth process is, of course,
theoretical. But it can give the therapist a feeling for what happens to a
family when its members are experiencing difficulty, where therapy en-
ters the picture, and what can be expected as a result of intervention. It is
important to note that much has happened to a family prior to therapeutic
intervention. Frequently, the therapist's efforts are viewed by the family
as a "last-ditch effort" to make the family "right." It can be helpful for
the family to realize that years of dysfunctional interacting cannot be
changed overnight. In some cases much time and effort must be expended
to produce satisfying results. It can be a long and difficult road from "C"
(the family's experiencing stress) to "I" (learning to resolve future
stress). But the results can seem worthwhile if family members can picture themselves at "D" (functional processing) or "I" for the rest of their
lives.

## General Personality Concepts

In order to identify functional and dysfunctional aspects of families,
it is necessary to discuss characteristics that all families have in common.
These characteristics are the ways and means that all family members
attempt to carry out their functions and meet their stated and unstated
goals. The discussion starts with general characteristics that are considered to be universal among families. It concludes with specific characteristics that relate directly to health and illness in individuals and family
groupings. The following five broad statements should give the reader a
feeling for the philosophical position of Integrative Family Therapy.

First, the family is a system. It is a network of specific interrelated
and interdependent parts. Each person in the family, as well as groupings
of individuals, is a part of the whole. Each individual is a separate part
of the system. But he or she is also another part of the whole each time

he or she joins with another member or members in a subgrouping. For example, the father is one part of the system because he is an individual in the unit. But he is also a second part of the system because he is in the parent subgrouping. He may also be other parts when he joins other individuals in subgroupings. In other words, each family member is at least one part of the system. Most likely, each family member is more than one part in the system.

The natural process of growth and development causes each part of the system to change. Even a slight change in any one part necessitates a change or realignment in the other parts. One can imagine the ramifications in a system if any one of its parts experiences major change. If the therapist is to truly understand and monitor the inner workings of the unit, he or she must be especially attuned to two facts: the multiplicity of parts, and the potential or actual consequences of change.

Second, a family is significantly influenced by aspects of its unique heredity and environment. Heredity refers to all innate biological elements of a person that are attributable to the genes of the parent. The environment is composed of all factors, besides genetic elements, that influence the growth and development of the individual. Society's reactions to ethnicity, race, and socioeconomic levels are significant parts of the environment.

Since each person responds differently to environmental influences, each member of the family has his or her own unique composition of environmental factors. In other words, no two people in the family internalize and process the same factors in any given situation. Since, from intrauterine life to death, environmental aspects are continually influencing an individual, these influences are considered by IFT theory to be more important than inherited elements of the person.

Third, all behaviors, attitudes, values, and feelings can be both rational (enhancing) or irrational (dysfunctional) to the individual or the family system. The context in which they are expressed is the determining factor. In one situation, a child's overt aggressive behavior may be totally inappropriate and considered to be unhealthy (e.g., in the classroom). The same behavior in a different context might be interpreted as an appropriate response (e.g., in an athletic contest). The key point is that behaviors, attitudes, values, and feelings do not possess inherent worth in and of themselves. They are not judged to be good or bad when examined out of context. The total situation must be taken into consideration when an evaluation is made. An individual's seemingly bizarre behavior may be an appropriate response to his or her particular family situation at that point in time. The same might be said for a total family's reaction to its environment. That which on the surface may seem to be irrational and dysfunctional may be an appropriate adaptational response. The therapist must avoid labeling or adopting a judgmental attitude without a close evaluation of the total situation. Behaviors, attitudes, values, and feelings cannot be adequately understood out of context.

Fourth, homeostasis is a desired state for all individuals and systems. As needs arise, tension is produced in the organism. The satisfaction of those needs reduces the tension and returns the system to a more balanced state. Thus, it is ideal if needs are appropriately satisfied and a comfortable balance is achieved. When needs are left unsatisfied, the tension remains in the system. Homeostasis is not achieved, and the organism must find other ways of returning to the balanced state. The goal of most alternative methods is to reduce tension, not satisfy needs. Therefore, frequently, these alternative methods are dysfunctional because they do not lead to the satisfaction of the original need. Neuroses and psychoses are common ways for individuals to achieve a temporary balance without actually satisfying the original need. Symptoms such as phobias, conversion reactions, and depression are an individual's personal homeostatic mechanism. A common balance mechanism for a family is to project the tension in the unit onto one of its members. Instead of the entire system being upset and unbalanced, it is an individual who is behaving in inappropriate ways. The homeostatic mechanism is therefore always dysfunctional, whether it occurs in an individual or in a system, since it can never achieve the ideal goal of need satisfaction. At best, the homeostatic mechanism can achieve a temporary unnatural reduction of tension. The tendency of individuals and families to trigger the homeostatic mechanism for the purpose of achieving balance at all costs must be continually countered by the therapist. For example, premature termination of counseling is a common homeostatic mechanism. The tension is necessary to keep the organism searching for appropriate satisfaction of its needs. The homeostatic mechanism will only postpone or temporarily avoid this quest.

Fifth, all behaviors of an individual or a system are attempts to preserve and enhance the organism. The goal is never to destroy. The result may be self-destructive, but the intent is always growth. With this in mind, all debilitating and harmful behaviors, attitudes, values, and feelings are distorted or misdirected attempts to save or to help the system. In other words, no organism has the capacity to willfully and knowingly produce self-destruction.

## Specific Personality Concepts

The following five specific characteristics are based on the preceding philosophical position of Integrative Family Therapy. They are the means by which the therapist develops his or her diagnostic picture of the family and its members. This evaluation should lead to an individualized treatment plan for the family, consisting of treatment goals, working hypotheses, and intervention strategies. Everything that is done in therapy should relate directly to these five specific characteristics.

1. FAMILY STRUCTURE  The first concept is a modification of the Structural model developed by Salvador Minuchin (1974). He focuses upon subsystems, describing them as being organized around family functions. The family decides who will participate and who will be excluded in the subsystems. Any combination of family members is allowed, particularly if their presence is viewed as important for the fulfillment of functions. A mother and son may work together to complete one task, while another would call for the alliance of father and son. The possible combinations of family members into subsystems is practically infinite. Therefore, the configuration of subsystems in any given family can easily become complex and confused. Integrative Family Therapy's focus is narrower, concentrating upon the three major subunits of a family: marital or adult, parental, and sibling. This focus illustrates the belief of Integrative Family Therapy that intragenerational alliances are more functional than intergenerational ones. Even though other alliances may be observed in family interactions, the therapist chooses to focus the majority of attention on these three subunits.

The marital subunit is composed of adult family members who are bonded together by emotional, sexual, or economic factors. It may encompass relationships involving the husband and wife in a nuclear or remarriage family or the single parent and a lover. This subunit is the source of adult-need satisfaction in the functional family. It is the adult support unit. In the dysfunctional family, it is frequently the arena of conflict, revenge, or avoidance. Typically, marital and sexual problems surface in this subunit. These conflicts may or may not affect the other subunits, depending on the type of boundaries that exist in the system.

The parental subunit is the governing body of the family. It is the source of decision making, goal setting, and nurturance for the entire unit. This subunit usually consists of the mother and father or any surrogate for these roles (e.g., step-parents, grandparents, or adult children). In single-parent families, the parental subunit may consist of only one adult. However, that parent may enlist the aid of another person to share in the functions of this subunit. A grandparent or older child may be included temporarily or permanently to help with the parenting and the decision-making functions. The parental unit functions best when the adults work as a team, communicating and coordinating their needs and wishes to accomplish the tasks of the unit. They are the executives in the family. It is important that they mutually guide the family. They ought not allow their directing of the family to be split or fragmented. Clear boundaries around this subunit function in two ways. First, they give privacy from undue outside influences. Second, clear boundaries permit appropriate interaction with the other subunits and with the outside world (particularly the extended family). The therapist will closely observe the workings of the parental team. And the therapist has the job of promoting mutuality and leadership throughout the therapy.

The sibling subunit is populated by the children of the family. This subunit is, in a sense, the training ground of the family. In a functional family the sibling subunit provides education, support, and guidance appropriate to the developmental levels of the individuals involved. Ideally, it helps to produce responsible and functional adults. In a dysfunctional family, it can be a place of considerable suffering and acting-out behavior. Thus, it is the source of many referrals for family therapy.

Family boundaries, as described by Minuchin (1974), are an integral part of the structure of the family. The family system should protect itself from, and be open to, outside influences from extended family and societal institutions. These clear boundaries allow the two-way flow of information and activity between the family and the outside world. Diffuse boundaries provide little protection from outside forces. These dysfunctional boundaries create an overinvolvement or enmeshment with outsiders. Rigid boundaries, on the other hand, provide maximum protection. Yet they shut out any influence from the outside. The result for the family is isolation and disengagement. This construct of clear, diffuse, and rigid boundaries is also applied to the subunits inside the family. Clear boundaries between the subunits and the individuals involved is considered to be the most functional arrangement. Clear boundaries are advantageous for the creation of mutuality and privacy, as well as the development of independence. Diffuse and rigid boundaries are always considered to be dysfunctional, except as temporary therapeutic strategies to effect change in the structure of the family.

2. COMMUNICATION AND PERCEPTION (C/P) The second concept, communication and perception, is a modification of the theory of Virginia Satir (1967). She emphasizes communication and perception as a total process. She does not specifically isolate the perceptive aspect as a source of dysfunction or as a focus of remediation. Barnhill (1979), building on Satir's work, discusses communication and perception as two parts of a process that he calls information processing. Therefore, his ideas are closer to Integrative Family Therapy than Satir's. The Integrative Family Therapist's emphasis, however, is particularly intensive in regard to the

perceptive element of the communication process. In fact, faulty perception is considered to be a more common dysfunction for families than is miscommunication.

The concept of communication and perception is perhaps the most important of the relationship dynamics because it pervades every personal interaction. All overt and covert human behavior involves communication and perception. We cannot survive in the world at any level of existence without communicating and perceiving on a moment-to-moment basis. None of the other characteristics can operate to their maximum capacity without accurate and clear communication and perception.

Since communication and perception are so vitally important, they are the eventual focus of almost every therapeutic encounter. The counselor may initially choose to realign subgroups in a family, or create greater role responsibility, or resolve a negative theme. But eventually, the concept of communication and perception will be an item of discussion and possible intensive intervention. In most cases, in order to maximize the fulfillment of functions, a family will need to make changes in their communication/perception process.

For example, a wife may send clear and concise messages to her husband. Yet, the husband may perceive these messages in an inaccurate and distorted manner, possibly because of his defensiveness. In this case, it is not the wife's communication that must be the focus of intervention but, rather, the husband's perception. A breakdown occurs in perception, which is the second part of the process. Thus, perception itself (e.g., defensiveness) can be the object of the therapist's energy. Preliminary research data on the Integrative Family Therapy model indicates that faulty perception is a more significant element in dysfunctional families than is faulty communication. According to this research, faulty perception occurred in 90% of the treatment families assessed. Poor communication was present in approximately 50% of the families in treatment (Walsh & Wood, 1983). This being the case, an Integrative Family Therapist would be more aware of each family member's perceptions, thereby possibly designing interventions to remediate the specific problem.

Communication, as previously stated, is the transmission of a message in any verbal or nonverbal manner. It is one aspect of a two-part process. Perception is the act of receiving that message. Thus, it is a different aspect of the process, and must be considered separately when the therapist is evaluating the complete communication/perception process. Clear communication is possible without accurate perception. But the reverse is very difficult to achieve. For example, one member can send a clear, distinct message accurately, while another receives a distorted message. The problem is not with the communicator, but with the perceiver. Hence, the focus of intervention is the perceiver. Asking the communicator to change his or her method of transmission may be ineffective, or even counterproductive. The emphasis should be upon more accurate perception by this one individual. On the other hand, if the problem is the transmission of mixed, double, or confused messages, the focus of intervention is quite different. By identifying the dysfunctional element—communication or perception—a more accurate treatment strategy will ensue.

Most families have consistent, characteristic methods of communication. They have an established process that varies little from incident to incident. Thus, if they are communicating inaccurately, the communication usually occurs the same way each time. In order to identify the patterns, the therapist can pose several questions: "How do people in the family communicate with one another?" "How do the family unit and the individual members communicate with outsiders?" "What are the channels of communication?"

Individuals may communicate and perceive differently within their family from the way they do with outsiders. Differences can more often be seen with communication than with perception. Usually, if an individual is perceiving inaccurately with family members, this problem is pervasive throughout all of his or her contacts. Accurate communication, on the other hand, can vary from situation to situation. Channels of communication refer to the individuals or groups that are usually involved in an interaction. If the sibling subgroup is communicating with the parental, which parent is usually chosen? Or are both chosen? When do the siblings go to Dad? When to Mom? Who handles communication with the school? Each situation may have to be explored depending upon the major themes that are presented or upon the roles that are established in the family. As the therapist and family interact, the therapist can begin to pinpoint specific incidents. Thus, it is possible to reorganize patterns in the therapy session. This reorganization usually occurs concurrently with other goals of therapy.

3. ROLE RESPONSIBILITY   A role is defined as the identity that a family member assumes, on a temporary or permanent basis, in order to complete certain tasks. A role, therefore, is a set of general and specific expectations that are accepted by or ascribed to each individual. These expectations may involve specific duties that must be performed on a regular schedule. Or they may be a general way of behaving with others. Since the completion of tasks is essential for a family to fulfill its various functions, appropriate expectations (role definition) and follow-through are particularly critical characteristics. Role responsibility is considered

appropriate when a certain sequence of events is followed. That is, when role responsibility is observed, individual expectations are clearly defined and articulated by the family. The role responsibilities are age appropriate and realistic for the individual. All members contribute to the definitions of their roles. In addition, each member accepts responsibility for his or her assigned duties. If the expectations are fulfilled, there are positive emotional, physical, or material consequences. When the expectations are not followed though, there are negative consequences. These may take the form of time-out or the removal of privileges. For role responsibility to be met, negative consequences are always geared to the age and developmental level of the family member.

This sequence is called the responsibility process. It is an aspect of the teaching/learning task of the family. And it is considered to be critical in the healthy development of individuals and families.

### Responsibility Process

| Expectations | Follow-through | Consequences |
| --- | --- | --- |
| clear | complete | clear |
| mutual | | mutual |
| realistic | | realistic |
| specific | | specific |
| consistent | | consistent |

A breakdown in any part of the process will eventually make it difficult, if not impossible, to fulfill family functions. At the very least, individuals will be dissatisfied with their own or others' behavior. The process involves all family members, whether adult, adolescent, or child. This is the specific characteristic that relates directly to one of the major problems in families, namely: role irresponsibility. The lack of clearly defined and articulate expectations for family members is a leading cause of disruption, particularly in adolescence. Certain behaviors may be assumed or taken for granted without ever being articulated. In other words, family members do not know what they should be doing or how they should be doing it. Any or all members can be placed in this position. A married woman may not know what her husband considers as a "good wife" (according to their personal definition of "good wife," of course). She may do what she considers best, but is frustrated and unhappy with her husband's negative reactions. The expectations are too general. They have probably not been discussed by the pair.

Parental attitudes about child rearing also fall into this category. Some parents feel that they are doing their children a favor by not giving them age-appropriate duties or by not requiring them to follow through on assigned tasks. These children are being raised as pampered, irresponsible children. The child's learned attitude and behavior usually carries over into the classroom and social activities.

Another, more insidious problem with roles involves the ascribing of individual roles, labeling of individual family members, or scapegoating of family members. By definition, these three issues involve lack of consent on the part of the individual. In this situation, a role, involving certain expectations, is given to an individual without choice or input. That person is then expected to follow through on the expectations. If he or she is unsuccessful, negative consequences will result. This situation is one of the most resistant to therapeutic effect.

Generally speaking, role irresponsibility is a result of one or more of the following:

**a.** Incomplete or general expectations.
**b.** Poorly articulated expectations.
**c.** Lack of personal input about expectations and consequences.
**d.** Inconsistent completion of expectations.
**e.** Lack of clear, appropriate consequences.
**f.** Ascribing, labeling, or scapegoating.

4. FAMILY THEMES   A theme is defined as any issue that occurs frequently for a family and that absorbs a significant amount of interest and attention of family members. These issues can be positive (growth enhancing) or negative (counterproductive or destructive). Issues are related to the psychoanalytic concept of the repetition compulsion. Positive themes involve the family in constructive activities that usually lead to growth for all family members. Positive themes are characterized by early resolution of conflicts and healthy channeling of tension toward goal accomplishment. Positive themes also demonstrate the family's resilience in problem solving. Family athletic pursuits, intellectual or cultural activities, and home maintenance are common examples of positive themes.

Negative themes, on the other hand, are characterized by nonresolution of conflict and increased tension. Whenever a particular issue related to the negative theme surfaces in the family, it creates disharmony and unhappiness. When negative themes are allowed to persist, the family is faced with unresolved conflicts that tend to multiply. The accumulation of these conflicts over many years can produce an irreconcilable situation. Individuals may decide to dissolve their family unit rather than work on this seemingly insurmountable list of grievances and conflicts. Common examples of negative themes include unsatisfactory academic achievement, role irresponsibility, differences in child-rearing practices, and generational attitudes about individual behaviors.

All families have several identifiable, major themes. These themes occur on a regular basis. Each usually involves similar dynamics when it reoccurs. Thus, for the family, major themes are like listening to the same record played many times. For negative themes in particular, the family is caught in a rigid pattern, compelled to repeat the same actions. In their experience of the situation, family members have little choice in how they will behave. As a result, they seek few alternatives. In the case of positive major themes, the family may choose to respond in a similar pattern each time the issue occurs. The difference is that members choose the behaviors because of the pleasure and growth the behaviors bring. The family members are not forced into patterns because of rigidity or absence of alternatives.

The therapist should attempt to identify the major positive or negative themes as soon as possible. Usually, several themes surface in the first two sessions. Negative themes generate the initial therapeutic goals for change. Negative themes involve those issues that most trouble the family on a daily basis. Resolution of these themes gives the family greater hope for continued change. In other words, the resolution of initial themes positively disposes the family to work on other, more resistant problems.

The feeling of relief that short-term change can produce may lead the family to premature termination. The therapist must be aware of this and work to counteract it from the first session. It appears that there are a limited number of negative themes in most families. Even in severely dysfunctional families, three to five negative themes are the norm. Also, positive themes should not be ignored or forgotten. It is important for the family to see the positive aspects of themselves while they are working to resolve the negative themes.

5. INDIVIDUAL PERSONALITY DYNAMICS (IPD). Personality dynamics refers to those strategies that an individual uses to organize, understand, and complete the tasks of daily living. Personality dynamics are the overt and covert means used for personal need satisfaction. Functional means lead to feelings of comfort and well-being (i.e., tension reduction). Dysfunctional dynamics distort or avoid reality in an attempt to attain immediate tension relief. Dysfunctional dynamics fail to satisfy the original need.

Including the concept of Individual Personality Dynamics in Integrative Family Therapy is a departure from the theories of most major family counseling models, although several family theorists attempt to account for individual psychologies in their formulations. Ackerman (1966), Kramer (1980), and Schwartz (1987), for example, consider individual family members to have personality dynamics that influence the family unit. These theorists believe that the intrapsychic phenomena for each family member affects the interpersonal processes in the family unit. However, each of these theorists has a specific theory of personality to understand and diagnose each family member. The Integrative Family Therapist also values intrapsychic phenomena, but feels that any individual model of therapy may be used in conjunction with the four relationship concepts. If this theory is to be useful to a variety of practitioners in different settings, why limit the choice of an intrapsychic model to one theory? Integrative Family Therapy offers the flexibility of choosing the individual model that best fits the individual therapist's philosophy of life.

Students of individual therapy models are familiar with the various explanations that theorists use to explain behavior. Psychoanalytic literature gives us one of the most well-developed theories for understanding behavior. Neo-analytic writers have expanded on Freud's thinking, producing an impressive array of concepts for explaining human behavior. During the past century, many other intrapsychic models of personality have developed, which are well-accepted in professional practice. The Integrative Family Therapist may choose from any one of these theoretical models. This flexibility is a particularly attractive option for the experienced therapist, who already has a well-developed personal model for understanding and treating individual problems. Thus, the options available to the Integrative Family Therapist for using various personality theories mean that a therapist may make a smooth transition from treating individuals to treating families. Integrative Family Therapists have used a number of the major individual models, including Rational-Emotive, Adlerian, Behavioral, Reality, Phenomenological, and Dynamic models.

The particular model chosen is less important than the fact that the therapist has a model for understanding intrapyschic dynamics. It is essential for the Integrative therapist to have an understanding of each family member's behavior in order to gain a complete diagnostic picture. It is important that the therapist have specific concepts for understanding individual behavior that are complementary to the concepts of family dynamics. Some Integrative Family Therapists choose to blend several intrapsychic models into an eclectic approach in order to understand the individual.

When the therapist begins to analyze the individual personality dynamics, it is the parents who should be considered first. They are the architects of this family. Thus, they have, in a sense, created some of the personality dynamics of their children. They are also the carriers of the dynamics from their own families of origin. For instance, the father's way of dealing with aggressive male behavior may be different from his wife's due to the different circumstances of their development in the family and society. Much parental behavior can be understood from an analysis of individual personality dynamics that were internalized by the husband and wife from their own families. These personality dynamics are transmitted to the children and are then employed in the current family for the development of family dynamics. The children, in turn, develop their own individual strategies for coping with each other and the outside world.

Individual dynamics are not significant factors in all therapeutic situations. In Integrative Family Therapy, they have been central to change in approximately 50% of the families seen in therapy.

It is the position of Integrative Family Therapy that individual personality dynamics alone are inadequate for understanding and explaining the myriad forces that affect family life. They may be used by the Integrative therapist in only some therapeutic situations. However, individual personality dynamics are an important ingredient in the mix of interpersonal relationships. As such, they are an essential piece of the entire family puzzle.

These five concepts constitute the theory of personality of Integrative Family Therapy. They represent the theoretical framework of the therapist from which all change strategies will emanate. All of the therapist's interactions with a family will be guided by the hypotheses generated from these constructs. The Integrative Family Therapist can gain a relatively complete diagnosis in two to three sessions. Information gained in these initial sessions is organized into the five categories. The therapeutic goals and methods of intervention are based directly upon this five-part diagnostic picture. Much of this information will be shared with the family. Their involvement in the process will be solicited by the therapist. A mutually motivated change process can then begin.

## THERAPEUTIC PROCESS

Integrative Family Therapy is a well-defined and structured process with a mean duration of ten sessions per family. It has specific stages, and each stage has certain tasks to accomplish. The therapist organizes the therapeutic encounter according to these stages and tasks, moving through them in an orderly fashion toward successful termination. Thus, this theoretical process provides direction for the therapist. Guideposts along the way help the therapist to evaluate the progress of the family. In actual practice, stages overlap and blend into one another as sessions flow from person to person or from topic to topic. The therapist might move from stage one to stage two and into stage three in a matter of minutes. He or she may then have to circle back to stage one in order to complete a structuring task. In other words, the live session does not always fit the organized theoretical pattern. Even so, for the Integrative Family Therapist, the theoretical pattern is essential for providing structure to a potentially disorganized and chaotic presentation of ideas, feelings, and behaviors. A family in conflict under varying degrees of tension and anxiety does not have the capacity to rationally evaluate what each member is saying, feeling, or doing. Nor can the members, under stress, take steps to remediate the situation. The therapist, with an organized theoretical process, does have the capacity to impose order, establish goals, and chart future directions. The point is that he or she has the cognitive structure of a theoretical process for a guide in each session.

The theoretical therapeutic process of Integrative Family Therapy consists of five relatively distinct stages. Each stage has specific tasks that must be accomplished before the family can effectively move to the next stage. Thus, the stages are developmental, in that, for each stage, the therapist prepares the family to move forward toward the tasks in the next stage. The five stages are organized so that a family can progress in an orderly fashion to accomplish the two major goals of Integrative Family Therapy. These are:

1. To remediate specific immediate difficulties and concerns of individuals and the family unit.
2. To build a satisfying problem-solving process that individual members and the family unit can use to deal with future problems.

These two goals reflect the two-fold emphasis of Integrative Family Therapy. Of initial importance is the resolution of present difficulties or crises that are sapping the day-to-day energies of the family. Setting and accomplishing short-term goals prepares and motivates the family to develop a more functional lifelong problem-solving orientation. Success in present-day problem solving inspires confidence and trust in the family's future potential. The removal of pain and the reduction in daily conflicts frees the family to devote more energy to long-range plans. Integrative Family Therapy's two goals are present in the mind of the therapist from the first session. The goals give the therapist direction from week to week.

## Stages in Therapy

1. STRUCTURING  The therapist asserts control from the beginning of the first session. This is not an authoritarian type of situation. It is instead an encounter between a professional with certain skills and a group of individuals (a family) who seek assistance regarding certain problem situations. It is a consultative type of relationship, which is analagous to that of an architect and a home builder or an accountant and a client. The therapist is employed by the family to assist the members in finding solutions to their individual and joint problems. It is never a power-related or adversarial relationship. The professional, by virtue of specific training and experience, has certain skills that are needed by the client. It is not a personal, social, or mystical relationship. In a sense, it is a businesslike arrangement that happens to involve intensely personal ideas, feelings, and behaviors. This is not to say that the therapist must be isolated and coldly analytical. On the contrary, mutual feelings of warmth, acceptance, and caring are essential for a productive therapeutic encounter. The therapist is in a unique and difficult position. He or she must maintain objectivity and separateness. But, at the same time, he or she is including himself or herself in the human drama of each family's life. Establishing and maintaining this type of relationship is the first challenge of therapy.

By exerting initial control, the therapist instills confidence and optimism in the family members regarding the potential for change to occur. There is order and stability in their lives, at least when they are in the session. The therapist's behavior also provides role models for individuals to emulate in the session and in their outside contacts.

In order to establish control, yet promote an accepting, cooperative atmosphere, the therapist has several critical tasks to accomplish in the first session. First, he or she should be firm about the overt parameters of their contractual relationship. For instance, he or she should establish a set time and length for their first few sessions. One-hour sessions are typical. Occasionally one and one-half hours are required for the first two or three weekly sessions. This is particularly true for a large or chaotic family, due to the structuring, organizing, and evaluating procedures that must take place. After the first few sessions, one-hour sessions on a weekly or biweekly basis may be appropriate.

The therapist should also request that all family members attend the first several sessions in order that he or she can observe how they interact, to introduce the entire family to the counseling process, and to gather information from all family members. Later sessions can involve any combination of individuals that the therapist deems necessary. The general idea, again, is that the therapist sets the initial limits (without being dogmatic) for their relationship. As a function of its pathology, a family may attempt to manipulate the therapist in these early stages. By being firm and consistent, the therapist can begin, very early, to restructure dysfunctional interactional behaviors. By vacillating, the therapist would allow the family to control his or her behavior. This would open the door for the family to resist interventions at a later date.

The second critical task is to make contact with each individual member and to elicit help and information from him or her. The therapist wants to communicate both his or her concern for the family and a willingness to accept it no matter what develops in their relationship. The classic concepts of therapeutic rapport are relevant at this point. Trust, acceptance, confidentiality, and unconditional positive regard are attitudes that the therapist communicates to each member in order to build rapport. Each individual should be led to feel both that what he or she says is important and that he or she is important to the success of the relationship.

The third critical task of the therapist is to model healthy communication/perception processes. He or she must be clear and specific in interactions with the family. And he or she must insist that family members behave this way also. The therapist should make sure that he or she understands what is being communicated by clarifying clients' statements and feelings on a regular basis. At the same time, he or she can teach family members to display good perceptive behaviors by asking them to clarify others' statements and give specific feedback to one another.

The three tasks outlined above are considered to be critical for a productive therapeutic relationship. These tasks are somewhat antagonistic to each other, in that the therapist is asked to behave in several potentially conflicting ways simultaneously. He or she is asked to be controlling, yet accepting, and to be individually oriented, yet concerned about the whole group. In one sense, these may be tasks that the family needs to accomplish. By demonstrating such a range of ways in which to be functional, the therapist can set the stage for later change. In other words, these tasks are critical to the therapist in order to manage future sessions successfully. But they are also important to the family because they may be behaviors that will be required of them in order to function more effectively in the future.

2. OBSERVATION AND ASSESSMENT   The second stage in the process involves an analysis of the family as a unit, and of each individual within the unit. It is essentially an evaluation of the specific and general dynamics that are present in each individual and in the unit. The therapist first attempts to identify and isolate specific problems that have propelled the family into therapy. These will be translated into short-term goals for the immediate future. Temporary resolution of the most pressing immediate concerns can free the family to deal with the more pervasive, general dysfunction that is causing them pain. The long-term goals relate specifically to this general dysfunction.

In order to be complete, this stage is of necessity multifaceted. Four phases can be identified. Each refers to a different yet related aspect of the family. One phase focuses upon the immediate presenting problems. In the first session, short-term goals may be discussed and established. These will deal directly with the most pressing problem. A second phase is the long-range remediation of general dysfunction that may be present in individual members or in the entire unit. Another phase involves evaluation of each family member's individual personality dynamics. The fourth phase is concerned with the dynamics of the unit as a whole. These phases are not isolated or progressive steps. They occur simultaneously and continuously in the beginning sessions. They are only discrete entities in the mind of the therapist. They serve as a constant reminder of the complexity of the interactions that he or she is observing. The phases represent different levels of involvement that all contribute to the dysfunctionality of the family. Each is essential for permanent change to occur and to be maintained.

The bases for observation and assessment in Integrative Family Therapy are the five specific characteristics of families. Using these concepts, the therapist develops a diagnostic picture of the entire unit. He or she can observe present interactions and evaluate past functioning, based upon this framework. An important element of this picture is the family's definition of its problem. How do family members evaluate the past and present situations? How do they propose to resolve their difficulties?

The major portion of this stage can be accomplished within the first two sessions with a family. The primary dynamics should be observable in this period of time. Short- and long-term goals should be established by the end of the third session. This evaluation will then be shared with the family in written and verbal form. Typically, an assessment card is given to each family member at the beginning of the third session. This card contains the therapist's suggestions for therapeutic goals in rank order of importance. The family is given time to read and digest the information. The family is then asked to react to the assessment and to the plans for future therapeutic contact. Mutual goals are set at this time. The remaining three stages of therapy are based upon the therapist's overall evaluation and interaction with the family regarding the assessment card. Thus, all therapeutic interventions will be guided by this session's evaluation and interaction with the family. This is not to say that the therapeutic plan is unchangeable. Continual reevaluation of the working hypothesis is prudent and advisable. If changes are necessary, they should be discussed with the family and instituted immediately. The presentation of the assessment card is the beginning of the intervention process. Thus, stage two flows naturally into stage three. The general concept of observation and assessment may be summarized by the following:

    **a.** Provides a diagnostic picture of individuals and of the unit.
    **b.** Establishes short-term and long-range goals.
    **c.** Determines present and future interventions.
    **d.** Is shared with the family in written form, then discussed by all members.
    **e.** Is accepted or modified by all persons in the session (family and therapist).
    **f.** Is flexible enough to incorporate new data as therapy progresses.
    **g.** Can change based upon the concept of continuous reevaluation.
    **h.** Is the start of the intervention process.

    3. INTERVENTION   Based upon the diagnostic picture that was developed in the second stage, the therapist begins to actively intervene in the family system. Theoretically, intervention cannot occur until the evaluation has been completed. However, in reality, the therapist begins the change process from the first session. The behaviors that he or she uses to structure a family and to assess dynamics are intervention strategies. His or her mere presence, as a professional, causes the family to interact in a different way. This difference in family patterns can be pointed out, thus creating change outside of the session. In other words, any contact that the therapist has with a family, or any of its members, is potentially an intervention.

    However, we can identify more specific techniques that the counselor can use to institute change. The following are the major intervention strategies of the Integrative Family Therapist.

    **a.** *The discussion and enactment of specific problem situations.*   Using recent examples of conflict situations, the therapist can provide a more objective analysis for the family, generating alternative solutions for its resolution. He or she can highlight critical incidents in the development and continuance of the problem. Frequently, this creates new insights for family members. They can now see alternative ways of behaving. From time to time, the therapist may have to actively interpret the dynamics of the situation. He or she may need to suggest specific new behaviors. Whether the therapist nondirectively guides or actively manipulates a situation is dependent upon the family's capacities and upon the theoretical orientation of the therapist.

If the family is unable to creatively resolve a conflict with the indirect help of the therapist, he or she must become more active and directive. In other words, the behavior of the therapist is somewhat dictated by the needs and capabilities of each individual family. He or she must be prepared to function differently with each family, or with the same family in different situations. In this way, he or she not only provides maximum assistance in specific situations, but also models flexible problem-solving behaviors. He or she is telling the family verbally and nonverbally, directly and indirectly, that different situations require different responses. Flexibility is a key element in harmonious, constructive growth.

**b.** *Use of confrontation techniques to help people communicate more accurately and effectively with one another.* The therapist encourages all family members to discuss all aspects of a situation openly and directly and discourages the continuance of hidden agendas and covert meanings in the communication/perception process. The therapist encourages all members to speak openly about their perceptions and reactions. By reducing the threat of reprisal or retribution, the therapist creates an atmosphere of trust and honesty. When threat is lowered, the need for protection and subterfuge is decreased.

**c.** *Use of communication checks to ensure accurate perception on the part of all family members.* Within the sessions, the therapist establishes a pattern of continually checking his or her perception of what has been communicated and encourages family members to do the same. Assumptions and inaccurate perceptions should be immediately identified and corrected. The family can be instructed to practice these behaviors at home, making them a permanent part of its members' interactional patterns. Checking one's perceptions is a learned behavior. The more practice a family has, the more likely it is to continue that behavior in the future.

**d.** *Working out definite roles and expectations for each member.* The therapist encourages all family members to identify both specific expectations they have for one another and specific tasks that are part of each other's roles. Individuals can negotiate aspects of their roles in order to achieve mutually satisfying positions. Consequences may have to be established for the noncompletion of tasks. The key element is mutuality. All members should feel that they have contributed to the establishment and maintenance of satisfying roles that are essential for the health of the unit.

**e.** *Helping the family set rules that will govern its members' daily interactions.* These rules can be very specific or general in nature. For example, family members should respect one another and listen to each other. More specific rules would include those concerning dating, having friends at the house, and curfew hours. It is up to the family members to decide how they want to organize their daily living patterns. Rules can give them well-established guidelines for a smooth organization.

**f.** *Encouraging the family to hold regular family meetings to supplement the therapeutic contacts.* Meeting structure and content can be rehearsed and reviewed in the therapy sessions. Initially, meetings can be used to practice and reinforce the new behaviors learned in therapy. In the later stages of therapy, the meetings will represent the major force for future change. Meetings can eventually take the place of the therapeutic sessions.

The preceding six techniques are the primary strategies of the Integrative Family Therapist. But they are not the only therapeutic tools used. Each counselor must develop his or her own repertoire to supplement those presented here. No professional can be expected to completely fit any one completely prepackaged therapeutic mold.

4. CHANGE MAINTENANCE   The primary task of the fourth stage of therapy is to reinforce new behaviors and patterns of interaction. The therapist may continue to use his or her intervention strategies. These will probably be used in a less active, less directive manner. The family is now taking more responsibility for members' present and future behavior. The therapist will increase the time between sessions, as the therapist gradually removes himself or herself from a central position in the family. Two- and three-week intervals between sessions are common in this fourth stage. The therapist can now help the family to generalize its new insights and behaviors to all aspects of its members' lives within and outside of the unit. They no longer focus all of their energy upon coping with present conflicts. A satisfying problem-solving process for the present

and future has emerged. The family is actively involved in planning for, and is more optimistic about, the future. However, the therapist must guard against moving too quickly through the fourth stage. Premature withdrawal of the therapist's influential position in the unit can trigger the homeostatic mechanism. Without the continued input and reinforcement of the therapist, a family can revert to old behavior patterns. Progressive movement through this fourth stage will decrease the likelihood of relapse.

5. REVIEW AND TERMINATION    Termination is indicated when a family is displaying the following behaviors:

a. Present-day conflicts are resolved in a mutually satisfying manner.
b. Members express optimism about future plans.
c. The family sets realistic long-term goals for the unit and for each individual member.
d. Each member has internalized the new behaviors, attitudes, and feelings.

When the therapist observes these behaviors occurring on a regular basis, termination can be instituted. The therapist should first review the family's entire therapy process and specifically reinforce the new behaviors and interactional patterns. He or she should then check each individual's feelings and attitudes toward the changes that have occurred. Has each member personalized and internalized the changes? Next, the therapist should discuss the future goals of the unit and of each member.

The final task of the therapist is to present written and verbal feedback to the family concerning his or her perception of its therapeutic process. This would include the initial presenting problem, assessment of the unit and individual members' goals, review of new individual and family behaviors, and an evaluation of the family's present functioning. It is suggested that this feedback be in written as well as verbal form, using the original assessment card as a basis, so that the family can review the therapist's evaluation at any time in the future. It is not unusual for families to review the feedback card at regular intervals. In this way, it provides continued reinforcement of therapy, long after formal counseling has ended. Four-week intervals between sessions in this last stage are the norm.

The stages of the therapeutic process are theoretical. They are part of the conceptual framework that is used both to organize the therapy process and to remediate dysfunctional families. The process itself is intensive and short-term. Most families complete the five stages in ten to twelve sessions spread over four to five months. Some families can reach termination in as few as five sessions over two to three months. Others require more extensive reorientation and may be in therapy for nine months to a year. Regardless of the duration, the theoretical process is essentially the same. Successful therapy, in other words, always follows the progression from structuring to termination with all the drama, pain, excitement, and pleasure of the intervening stages.

## BIBLIOGRAPHY

Ackerman, N.W. (1966). *Treating the troubled family*. New York: Basic Books.

Barnhill, L.R. (1979). Healthy family systems. *Family Coordinator* 28, 94–100.

Minuchin, S. (1974). *Families and Family Therapy*. Cambridge, MA: Harvard University Press.

Satir, V. (1967). *Conjoint Family Therapy*. Palo Alto, CA: Science and Behavior Books.

Schwartz, R. (1987). Our Multiple Selves. *Family Therapy Networks,* 11(2), 24–31.

Walsh, W.M. (1989). Twenty major issues in remarriage families. Unpublished manuscript at University of Northern Colorado. Submitted for publication.

Walsh, W.M., and Wood, J.I. (1983). Family assessment: Bridging the gap between theory, research, and practice. *American Mental Health Counselors Journal* 5, 111–120.

# PART II

# Families with Young Children

# CHAPTER 1

# Too Close for Comfort: Stepfamily

PAUL FARINA
WILLIAM M. WALSH

Therapists: Paul Farina
Bonnie Guerra
Supervisor: William M. Walsh

## I. IDENTIFYING DATA

Dirk Connolly, age thirty-four, and Molly Connolly, age forty-two, have been married for one year. Prior to their marriage they had lived together for two years. This living arrangement had begun shortly after Molly was divorced from her first husband. Dirk had been divorced for five years prior to meeting Molly three and one-half years ago. His ex-wife lives in another part of the country with their daughter, Melanie, age ten. Molly's three children live with her and Dirk in a three-room apartment in a large city. The children sleep in the bedroom, while Dirk and Molly sleep in the living room. The children are Amanda, age nine; Jimmy, age seven; and Curt, age five. The children have periodic contact with their father, who lives in the same city. Dirk is a full-time student at a local private

**31**

college. He also works part-time. Molly is a preschool teacher in a city school. The three children attend a local public school.

## II. INTRODUCTORY MATERIAL

Dirk called the clinic to request an appointment for his family. He had been referred by a counselor at his college whom he had consulted for "excess stress." He stated that he had been under a great deal of pressure lately from school and home. He was in his junior year at college. He found being an older student among traditional college-aged students difficult. He also indicated that the family was experiencing difficulty "adjusting to each other" and added that the children were not responding to him as "father." He agreed with the college counselor that the entire family needed to participate in the counseling process.

## III. INFORMATION GATHERING (SESSIONS 1 AND 2)

At the beginning of the first session the therapists introduced themselves and led the family to the counseling room. The chairs were arranged in a horseshoe configuration, and the family was allowed to seat themselves. The three children sat together from left to right. Then came Molly, and next to her sat Dirk. After everyone was comfortably seated, the therapists briefly explained the therapy process, including the videotaping, the use of the phone, and the requirement for a three-session commitment. After the ground rules had been explained, family members were asked to introduce themselves. The two older children started by mentioning their grade in school and what they liked to do there. Curt had moved to his mother's lap and had fallen asleep, clutching his stuffed elephant. Therefore, he did not introduce himself. Although the heating system appeared to be working satisfactorily, the children kept their coats on throughout the entire session.

Dirk responded next. He briefly described his workload at school and home. He was articulate but soft-spoken and seemed to carefully consider his words before speaking. He appeared to be tired. He spoke in a labored voice and rubbed his eyes frequently. He described recent events—the coming of the end of the semester and finals—in a manner that indicated that he was under much stress. He informed the group that he had a daughter from his previous marriage and that she was living in another state. He could not remember much about raising her, but he did mention that she was spoiled and that his ex-wife had not been very strict with her. When speaking of Molly's children, he made it a point to say that he was not the children's real father.

The therapists then shifted the discussion to Molly and Dirk. They asked how the couple had met and what their early relationship had been like. Amanda immediately volunteered to tell the story. Molly perked up and seemed interested to hear her daughter's version, but she interrupted along the way, correcting the accuracy of the chronology and content.

Molly had been divorced from her first husband for only a few months when she met Dirk. She recalled that her first marriage had been "on the rocks" for a long time. She said that her ex-husband was an abusive alcoholic who was very strict and stern. She frequently felt the need to protect the children from him. She strongly stated that the marriage had been over long before she had actually gotten the divorce.

At this point the therapists inquired about the presenting problem in order to understand what had brought this family to counseling. Molly indicated that she was concerned about the fighting among the children. "I was an only child, and I don't know how to deal with sibling rivalry." She also felt that there was no clear line of authority in the household and that the situation had gotten out of hand. She added that the children, especially Jimmy, went around pointing at either Molly or Dirk and saying, "You're not the boss." Dirk reported that he had become very upset when he saw Molly being verbally abused by the children. He stated that he had even seen Molly being slapped on a few occasions. However, he had been hesitant to interfere as he was "only" the children's stepfather. He said that the situation had become so urgent that he had resorted to threatening the children with a spanking if they didn't obey his directives. He claimed to have gotten "results" even though he had not yet spanked anyone. He again expressed confusion about his role in the family and seemed unsure about how the children viewed him. During Dirk's entire testimony, Jimmy covered his face with his hat. When Amanda and he were questioned about Dirk's role in the family, they stated that they usually called him "Dirk" and not "Dad."

Dirk indicated another problem area when he said that he didn't feel that the children had a sense of responsibility. He used as an example the fact that the children didn't clean their own room. Molly stated that it was easier to clean the room herself than to get an unpleasant response.

One of the therapists questioned the couple as to whether they had talked about what a clean room should look like and what the children should be doing to make it look that way. Molly responded that they had not. Later they were asked how it was established as to who does what between the two of them. Dirk replied, "It seems to work out that I do this, she does that. We never discuss it—it just seems to balance out."

The therapists then shifted the focus of the session to Dirk and Molly's marriage. Both complained that they had neither the time nor the money to go out together. Dirk did express, however, that he liked spending time with Molly and that things would be a lot easier if there were not "so much anarchy." It also appeared that they did things together as a family very infrequently. Molly shared that her suggestions for family outings were consistently shot down by the children.

When questioned about the procedure used when the children fought, Molly explained that she sent them to their room. Then she would try to find out who had done what to whom. In describing a typical day, Dirk mentioned that there was no routine at all after school, that it was just "come what may."

As the session came to a close, the therapists gave the couple a homework assignment to work on during the week. They were asked to think about other family concerns. They were also requested to formulate a list of expectations that they had for the family. Since both were school-oriented, the therapists had a strong hunch that they would follow through on their homework!

The therapists also pointed out that there was a strong bond of love in the family and that Dirk and Molly seemed motivated to change. Since adequate data for the assessment card had been gathered from the children, the therapists asked that only Molly and Dirk come to the next session, so that the focus could be on their relationship.

Dirk and Molly came to the second session with their list of expectations for the family. Dirk indicated that he wanted the children to be more honest. He gave as an example the situation where the children have been fighting and he attempts to get to the bottom of what happened, but the children won't tell him the truth. As a result of this, Dirk said that he became confused as to how to handle the situation and uncertain about whom to punish. He added that, if he attempted to discipline Jimmy, Jimmy would respond, "You're not my father." One of the therapists emphasized that, even though Dirk was not Jimmy's biological father, he was Jimmy's parent and, as such, was responsible for parenting him.

The therapists then acknowledged the work the couple had done in preparing their list of expectations. Because the content of the list was quite general, Molly and Dirk were directed to talk with one another about their specific expectations for the children. They were also asked to come up with a plan of action if the children did not fulfill those expectations. They seemed to have much difficulty in developing and agreeing on specific expectations and consequences. Dirk doted on reasons why certain consequences wouldn't work, while Molly gave very little input. She explained to the therapists that she repeatedly told the children what she wanted them to do and why. She was asked how she handled her students at school. She admitted that she was "swallowed up" by students above the fourth grade and that she was more comfortable with preschoolers and lower grade students, because the younger ones did not challenge her authority.

The therapists redirected Dirk and Molly to the task at hand—developing clear expectations and consequences for their children. After much communication and direction from the therapists, the couple finally agreed that each wanted the children to clean up their rooms. They had not yet come up with a consequence for lack of follow-through on this expectation. The therapists explained to them that it was not necessary to have the same consequence for each of the children, even though they might all have the same expectation.

Dirk and Molly then brought up another issue, that of the children's screaming and yelling in the car. They found this behavior annoying and distracting. They said it was not a problem when the children were involved in a game or activity. The therapists encouraged them to set up expectations and consequences around this issue also.

The therapists then followed up on a subject that had been mentioned in the previous session, alcoholism. The couple was asked what role it played in the family. Dirk responded that he had a drinking problem and had gone through treatment twice about five years ago. He reported that he had attended AA several times a week during his early recovery but that he had not been to a meeting in several months. However, he did feel that he was still working on a recovery program. Since he had been sober for five years, he no longer considered drinking to be one of his coping strategies. He also mentioned that he tended to be compulsive and perfectionistic.

As the session came to a close, the therapists gave the couple their homework assignment. They were to talk together (without any input from the children) and come up with two expectations and two consequences for each of the children. Then they were to implement them immediately. They were also to decide on a fun activity for the entire family and act on it. They were reminded that they would be receiving their assessment cards in the next session and that the entire family should be present.

## IV. INTEGRATIVE EVALUATION

**Structure:**


**Roles:**


**Communication/Perception:**


**Themes:**


**Individual Personality Dynamics:**

## V. FAMILY ASSESSMENT CARD

The assessment of your family's strengths and weaknesses is based on observation and clinical evaluation by your therapists in consultation with the supervisory staff.

The assessment will provide important information for your family. A commitment by each family member to work on mutually agreed-upon goals both in the sessions and at home between the sessions will maximize the value of this assessment. Work on each of the goals will help your family to function more effectively and help each family member to change and grow.

_____

_____

_____

_____

_____

_____

_____

_____

_____

_____

_____

_____

_____

_____

_____

_____

# VI. COMPLETED INTEGRATIVE EVALUATION

**Structure:**
Diffuse boundary between the parental and sibling subunits; parents not working as a team; diffuse boundary between marital and parental subunits—neither unit clearly defined

**Roles:**
*Expectations:* Unclear, not specific, neither determined nor stated
*Consequences:* None that work; screaming, threatening, abdicating
*Follow-through:* nonexistent

**Communication/Perception**
*Communication:* Assumptions, arguing, overexplaining, lack of directness, better listening needed by all
*Perception:* Periodic defensiveness by adults

**Themes:**
Irresponsibility by Dirk and Molly toward parental roles; chaotic family—lack of chain of command; role confusion; recovery from alcoholism; lack of adult time; lack of family time

**Individual Personality Dynamics:**
*Dirk:* Neat, compulsive, withholds feelings, explosive, perfectionistic
*Molly:* Overprotective of children, childlike, extremely passive in use of authority
*Jimmy:* Possibly hyperactive, resentful of authority

## VII. COMPLETED FAMILY ASSESSMENT CARD

> The assessment of your family's strengths and weaknesses is based on observation and clinical evaluation by your therapists in consultation with the supervisory staff.
>
> The assessment will provide important information for your family. A commitment by each family member to work on mutually agreed-upon goals both in the sessions and at home between the sessions will maximize the value of this assessment. Work on each of the goals will help your family to function more effectively and help each family member to change and grow.
>
> 1. Parents need to have clear and specific expectations for the children.
> 2. Follow-through on parents' expectations for children needs to be complete.
> 3. Consequences need to be clear, specific, appropriate, and consistent.
> 4. Praise or some other kind of positive reinforcement should to be given when children's follow-through is complete.
> 5. Molly and Dirk need to work as a parental team.
> 6. Molly and Dirk need to strengthen marital subunit by getting involved in adult-only activities.
> 7. Molly and Dirk need to lessen assumptions by using perception checks.
> 8. Molly needs to make clear, direct statements to the children and avoid overexplaining.
> 9. Family members need to listen to and understand what the other person is saying before responding.

## ASSESSMENT SESSION (SESSION 3)

When everyone was seated, the therapists gave each of the family members (except Curt) an assessment card. As the therapists reviewed the card, they made sure to reinforce the family members for their good communication, their openness, and their willingness to work on family problems.

While discussing the point about communicating expectations and consequences to the children, one of the therapists stressed to Molly how unproductive it was to overexplain. In reference to the fourth item on the card, Dirk and Molly admitted that they had not been giving much positive reinforcement to the children. Molly stated that she didn't think it was necessary to reward the children for tasks that they were expected to do on a regular basis. Dirk seemed to disagree. After pondering it, Molly said that she thought that they did verbally praise the children on occasion. But she believed that she and Dirk were so geared up for resistance that they forgot about positive reinforcement.

During this discussion Dirk was quieter and seemed somewhat tired. He explained that he had been keeping very late hours studying for exams. He added that he was looking forward to having time off during spring break and was hoping to spend some of it with Molly.

After reviewing the assessment card and discussing the dynamics of the Integrative Model, the therapists focused on the homework assignment from the previous week, encouraging the couple to continue their dialogue about expectations and consequences. As Dirk and Molly attempted to reach mutual agreement on clear and specific expectations for the children, the therapists noticed how bored Amanda looked. Jimmy sat in his mother's lap as the discussion between the parents continued. One of the therapists asked him to sit on the opposite side of the room. He silently obeyed. Toward the end of the session it was explained to the parents that this had been done in order to clarify the boundary between the parental and sibling subunits. It was further explained that the couple's discussions and decisions as parents did not need to involve the children.

The therapists continued to observe the interactions of Molly and Dirk as they struggled to arrive at expectations for their children. They refocused the couple whenever either of them jumped topics or looked for reasons why certain expectations were inappropriate. At one point Molly was talking to Jimmy about a consequence for Curt when she should have been talking to her husband! The therapists redirected her. Although the process that the couple used was frustrating to watch, their work did pay off in that they finally arrived at some clear and mutually agreed-upon expectations.

At one point in the process Amanda complained that she was bored. The look on her brothers face mirrored that sentiment. The therapists were pleased to see this, as they felt it was an indication that the parents were maintaining a clear boundary between themselves and the children. It also showed that the children were not interested in hearing about limits being set on their previously unstructured behaviors.

As the session came to a close, the therapists reinforced the efforts of the parents. For homework they were directed to continue to set time aside to talk together to reach agreement on further expectations and consequences for the children. Because the Connollys were highly motivated and were proceeding at a very fast rate, the therapists requested that they return in two weeks, confident that the extra week between sessions would not hinder the family's progress. They also requested that only Dirk and Molly attend the next session.

## IX. SUBSEQUENT SESSIONS

The Connollys arrived on time for session four and made themselves comfortable in the therapy room. Dirk crossed his legs, lit his pipe, and took a sip from his coffee cup. The therapists questioned the couple about their homework assignment. Molly and Dirk said that they had spent time talking over expectations and consequences and that, in general, things were working out better. Everyone had a good laugh when Dirk related that Jimmy had said, "I have to do everything you say now." It was felt that this comment indicated how Jimmy viewed his parents' progress!

When asked for specific information, Molly pulled a piece of paper from her purse. It was a list of expectations and consequences in the following areas: the children's snack time; eating a nourishing dinner; picking up their room every day; and cleaning their room on Saturday. The therapists felt that both the expectation and consequences were clear and age-appropriate. Molly had been careful not to make the language too difficult for Curt to understand, and she stated that Amanda and Jimmy were willing to help explain the new rules to him.

Dirk stated that he now felt more responsible for his own behavior, since he was attempting to provide a role model for the children. But despite an obvious decrease in the degree of chaos in the household, Dirk and Molly were feeling quite helpless about Jimmy's behavior. Dirk described Jimmy as a "habitual liar" and stated that Jimmy had recently stolen a neighbor's remote control device. Both parents were confused about what consequences they should impose for this behavior. Molly also reported that she had transferred Jimmy to the school where she taught, so that she could more closely monitor his behavior and progress. She also felt that he had not been challenged sufficiently in his other school and had not been challenged sufficiently in his other school and had seemed bored most of the time. The therapists shared with the Connollys their impression of Jimmy—that he did indeed appear to be quite bright and seemed to have a very active imagination. Molly mentioned that his teacher had said the same thing. The therapists attempted to help the couple see Jimmy's positive attributes and to normalize his behavior. Dirk was insightful in realizing that, by anticipating Jimmy's undesirable behaviors, the parents might be sending a message to him that undesirable behavior was what they expected of him. This led to another discussion concerning the need for Dirk and Molly to reinforce their children's positive behavior.

At this point in the session, the therapists brought up a topic that had concerned them since the first session, Dirk's feeling like a nonparent in the family. Dirk was asked if this had changed at all. He answered that, before, he had felt that he was just an authority figure and a disciplinarian, but that now he felt he was a constructive part of the children's lives. He added that he had blamed Molly's ex-husband for the way the children had been behaving but that now, as an active parent, he felt that he was able to provide structure for the children, thereby changing their behavior. Furthermore, some of his fears had been allayed when he realized that the children continued to be affectionate toward him even though he had been structuring them much more than he had previously.

The therapists recognized the work the couple was doing as a parental team and complimented the two on their open communication. They also commented on the fact that the couple continued to maintain a clear boundary between the parental and sibling subunits. Molly and Dirk replied that they were more frequently going off to a room by themselves, away from the children, when they wanted to consult with one another. It was noted that they now seemed to be truly sharing the responsibility for parenting. Molly stated that she sensed the degree of commitment that Dirk had toward her and the family. Dirk stated that he would not be able to parent without Molly. The therapists were pleased to see this mutual interdependence and appreciation.

Since the parental subunit seemed to be functioning more effectively, the therapists decided to access the marital subunit. Molly explained that, as husband and wife, she and Dirk were now communicating more on an emotional level. She then expressed to Dirk how hurt she had been about a remark that he had made about leaving her if she ever got pregnant again. This touched off an issue, Molly's fear of Dirk's leaving the relationship, that would be further explored in a later session. Dirk stated than in his previous marriage he had rarely expressed feelings at all. He claimed to be doing much more expressing with Molly. However, they still were not doing enough enjoyable things together as a couple to help nurture their marriage. Dirk blamed this lack on the stresses of school, his father's living with them temporarily, and their cramped living quarters. He felt that all of these things were making it difficult for him and Molly to attend to their personal needs. He also claimed to have tunnel vision where school was concerned, blocking out all other personal needs. (The therapists saw this as an indication of Dirk's obsessive-compulsive streak.)

At the end of the session the couple was once more assigned homework. They were to (1) find a way to give the children more positive reinforcement, (2) make a list of expectations that they had for themselves as parents, and (3) continue to set consequences for the children and implement them. The next session was scheduled for two weeks. Amanda and Jimmy were to attend.

In the next session Molly and Dirk reported that Jimmy's consequence for stealing was that he did not have TV privileges for two weeks. Dirk still seemed very concerned about him and still referred to him as a compulsive liar. He had been wondering if he and Molly should seek some other kind of professional help for their son. The therapists began to worry that Jimmy might become the family's "identified patient." They made it clear that they did not think that Jimmy needed additional professional help and that his parents needed to be more consistent with him. They also said that they did not think the behavior the parents were describing was abnormal for a boy of seven.

Attempting to shift the focus of the session to the positive, the therapists inquired about how things had changed for the better. The Connollys reported that the children had been cleaning up their room every evening before dinner and that the snacking plan they had set up seemed to be working well. Molly added that the children were fighting a lot less among themselves. The therapists commented many times that the couple was doing well and seemed to have things under control much more than in previous weeks. But they also noticed that both Molly and Dirk tended to look at what was going wrong rather than at what was going right. They were still troubled by the fact that Jimmy continued to be verbally and physically abusive to Molly. Dirk indicated that he responded to this behavior by getting angry and subsequently spanking Jimmy. However, Dirk was aware that he had been getting hooked emotionally and that spanking Jimmy did not decrease the undesirable behavior. It was explained to Dirk that if he told Jimmy what was expected of him and followed through with a planned consequence, there would be no need for him to become emotionally involved. He would simply put his plan into operation. It was also mentioned that changing Jimmy's behavior depended greatly on rewarding him for desirable behavior rather than just punishing him for transgressions.

Since Molly and Dirk had planned to spend a weekend without the children, the therapists also inquired about how the weekend had gone. They reported that they had spent the weekend at a friend's house in the suburbs and had had a good time. However, near the end of their stay they had received a phone call reporting that Amanda had been "molested" by a friend of the baby-sitter. The couple did not go into great detail about the incident, and Amanda declined to speak about it when questioned by the therapists. The therapists assumed that "molested" meant sexually abused, but the parents did not mention whether or not they had reported the incident to the authorities. They did say that they had discussed it within the family. The therapists surmised that Dirk and Molly were feeling a certain amount of guilt about leaving the children over the weekend. But they decided to let the issue pass for the moment, determined to pursue the details of the incident with vigor at the next session, when Dirk and Molly would be present without the children.

The following session was scheduled for two weeks later. For homework the Connollys were directed to come up with fun activities that they could do with the children, as well as activities that they would do apart from the children to strengthen their marital subunit.

A week prior to the next session, the therapists telephoned the Connollys to gain more information regarding the allegations of molestation. Dirk stated that he believed Molly had consulted with the pastor of their church and had reported the incident to the legal authorities. Dirk also stated that Molly had reacted to the incident more strongly than had Amanda, becoming physically ill for several days.

During the sixth session the therapists moved directly to the incident of Amanda's abuse. Molly did most of the talking and was visibly upset as she recounted the story of what had happened that weekend.

She stated that she and Dirk had left Amanda with a friend. But the friend had gone out on Saturday night and left the children with a friend of hers. Supposedly, the person was someone trustworthy. Molly then recounted what Amanda had told her. Another little girl, Amanda's friend, was also in the house. The man who had been left to baby-sit got into bed with both the girls and started to put his hand up Amanda's nightgown. Amanda, alarmed and angry, got out of bed and left the room. The other girl, who was younger than Amanda, had stayed in bed and was fondled in the genital area. Molly stated that she had praised Amanda for her behavior, reinforcing that she had done the right thing in leaving and that she should do it again if the same thing were ever to happen. Both Dirk and Molly then stated that they had not reported the incident to the authorities. Molly said that she had deliberated awhile and then had consulted with the pastor of their church and with the social worker at Amanda's school. They had discovered that the perpetrator was an illegal alien, and they were attempting to have him deported.

Molly appeared very upset throughout the session. The therapists noticed that she repeatedly interrupted Dirk, cutting him off and overtalking. It seemed that Dirk had not participated much in the whole incident regarding Amanda. He sounded vague and uninformed about important details of the episode. The therapists questioned him about his apparent passivity and wondered why he had not been taking equal parental responsibility around this issue. Dirk described his role as being supportive of Molly. He also felt that Molly had been handling the incident adequately and did not need his help. He said that he had talked with Amanda and had assessed that she was doing all right. He added that the matter had not affected Amanda's relationship with him. As the therapists confronted Dirk about not taking a more active role in the abuse incident, Molly tended to protect Dirk from this criticism. She claimed that he had shared enough of the responsibility with her and that she had noted his support after she had informed him of her activities relative to Amanda.

Although the greater part of the session had been spent researching the incident involving Amanda, the therapists did follow up on the couple's homework assignment of setting expectations and consequences around Jimmy's abusive behavior. The Connollys had not developed any ideas. Dirk had continued to get angry with Jimmy and to spank him as a punishment. Both parents seemed stuck about this problem. They seemed to get hooked by Jimmy much more easily than by the other children. Molly recognized this, stating that there were a "whole lot of different emotions wrapped up" when she dealt with Jimmy. One of those emotions was guilt. Both Dirk and Molly talked about the "look" that Jimmy gave them and continued to label him as the monster of the family. Somehow, they could not let go of their view of him as the identified patient.

Toward the end of the session, the therapists were pleased to hear about an area in which Dirk and Molly had taken better control. Molly's ex-husband planned to visit the children every Sunday. But he frequently missed visits, never giving advance notice that he would do so. So Dirk and Molly had decided to make an alternative plan each Sunday, just in case he didn't show up. That way, they were able to eliminate the feeling of being controlled by him.

At the end of the session it was mentioned again that Dirk's father had temporarily moved in with the family and was sleeping in the bedroom with the children. Because of the lateness of the hour, this topic was not pursued at that time.

For homework the therapists directed the couple to continue to attempt to set up expectations and consequences around Jimmy's disrespectful and abusive behavior.

At the next session both Molly and Dirk wore blank expressions on their faces when they were asked about the progress they had made on their homework assignment. Apparently, they had not made much progress. Molly mentioned an interesting piece of dialogue that she had had with her son. Jimmy had pointed out to his mother that whenever Amanda misbehaved she was told to do a written assignment as punishment. But when he, Jimmy, misbehaved, he was not given any punishment at all. Both therapists smiled in simultaneous understanding. They explained to the Connollys that Jimmy was asking to be treated as an equal sibling, rather than as the "monster" of the family. He was asking his mother to set consequences for him. Neither Dirk nor Molly responded to the therapists' explanation. Dirk sat with his arms folded tightly across his chest. Molly looked anxious.

The therapists, sensing that something was going on, questioned the couple. They explained that on the way over to the session that evening, Dirk had blown up about the condition of their apartment and the fact that he was unable to have any time alone in his own home. He was also angry about several other issues, which he proceeded to discuss in the session. The children were not cleaning their rooms or following orders. His father was still living with the family and seemed to be procrastinating about finding his own apartment. The apartment was too small for all of them, and Dirk only had quiet time for himself when the children were asleep. He never had time to sit, relax, and watch TV but was always studying or doing school work. As Dirk continued for about ten minutes, Molly offered no response.

The therapists then directed Molly and Dirk to communicate with one another so that they could observe the couple's communication patterns. Dirk described how he had lived before meeting Molly. He stated that he always had a neat, clean, quiet, organized environment in which to work. He expressed his commitment to Molly and the children but stated that he felt angry and disgusted with their current living situation. He threatened to leave if the situation continued to be so disorganized.

The therapists wondered whether this explosion was a periodic phenomenon. They said that they realized that Dirk experienced pressure and stress from school as well as from home and held his anger and frustration inside. Molly said that she was used to Dirk's venting in this fashion every month or so. She stated that she dealt with this behavior by either seeking solutions to the problems or by attempting to justify Dirk's feelings. She also said that when she made suggestions to Dirk about how he might have more privacy, he usually answered with "yes, but. . . ." The therapists urged Molly to respond to her husband on a feeling level. But she continued to sit quietly as Dirk angrily expressed his desire to leave and to live on his own again. He mentioned that they had previously separated for a short time and that they both agreed they could live without one another, if necessary. After further prodding from the therapists, Molly admitted that she was feeling hurt and defensive. She said she felt angry at Dirk for his threatening to leave. The therapists indicated that the couple needed to communicate their feelings to each other, even though it was painful. Molly cried while attempting to communicate with Dirk; Dirk had difficulty making eye contact with Molly. He anticipated her responses before she had a chance to speak. For homework they were asked to spend fifteen to twenty minutes a day communicating on both a content and feeling level. The session ended with Molly, teary-eyed, asking Dirk for a hug and Dirk responding affectionately.

The eighth session took place two weeks later. Molly and Dirk immediately began to talk about all the changes they had made in their apartment. They had decided to get rid of all the "junk" they didn't need anymore and had also folded up a table that was just taking up space. They had arranged to have their own private bedroom with a door that closed. It was the first time since they had been married that they had that kind of privacy. They were amazed at the difference it made. They reported that their sex life had improved and that Dirk was finally able to get his need for time alone met without leaving the house. The therapists were impressed with the way the couple had worked together to set physical and structural boundaries around their marital subunit.

The therapists asked the couple about the stresses in their lives and the effect those stresses might be having. Dirk recognized that it was possible that the stresses could become so great that he might return to drinking. For that reason he had decided to begin attending AA meetings regularly, stating that they had been helpful to him in the past. Molly and Dirk were asked to identify specific, stressful elements in their lives and the ways in which they were dealing with them. Molly stated that financial worries and the children produced the most stress for her. Dirk replied that, for him, it was school and the disorganization at home.

At this point in the session, the supervisory team made a phone call to the therapists, asking them to initiate a fantasy exercise around the notion of stress and problem solving. Dirk and Molly were to think of a story or parable that represented their problem. Then they were to continue with the fantasy to discover what might happen. Finally, they were to describe a solution to their fantasy, thereby describing a possible solution to their real-life situation. The purpose of this activity was to take the problem from a "stuck" reality to a reality in which resolutions were possible.

Molly began. She closed her eyes and relaxed for awhile, then started to talk about seeing herself as a bag lady walking along a busy city street. All alone, she would walk around, speaking to people passing by but not to anyone in particular. She explained that the bags contained stressful situations, which she kept trying to get rid of so as to lighten her load. Then she described getting on a bus to visit her grandchildren out West somewhere. She sat down next to a woman with a baby and had a nice conversation with her. The therapists asked her about the solution to her fantasy. Molly stated that she had a nice visit with her grandchildren; they made her feel loved and wanted. This feeling of being loved and cared about was extremely important to Molly. The therapists asked her if Dirk were in the fantasy at all. She said that he was not.

Then Dirk described his fantasy. He saw himself as a bear, feeling cooped up in his cave and yearning to go out and explore the wilderness. Periodically, he would feel like he was suffocating and needed to get out for awhile. He said that Molly was also a bear in the cave, either a panda bear or a teddy bear. The therapists asked Molly and Dirk to get up and act out this fantasy. Dirk seemed stiff, uncomfortable, and self-conscious. After much coaxing, he did a few turns, then went toward Molly and gave her a hug. He repeated this a few times to show how, on occasion, he felt close to Molly, but sometimes he also looked away, not paying any attention to her. Dirk had no solution to his fantasy. The therapists saw it as a reiteration of what Dirk had been saying in the counseling sessions.

Following the exercise, the therapists spoke to the couple about how Dirk's fantasy fed into Molly's fears and insecurities. She was alone in her fantasy but wanted love, support, and caring. In Dirk's fantasy, he kept leaving the cave and coming back. Therefore, Molly had to keep picturing herself on her own, because she couldn't be sure that Dirk, her big old bear, was going to stick around. Molly and Dirk both commented on the new insights that this experience produced for them.

At this point in the therapy process, the therapists felt that the Connollys had been in the change-maintenance stage for some time and were moving toward termination. They reinforced the importance of the couple's working with the tools they had, in order to come up with a workable plan to alleviate stress. The couple was asked to return in a month and told that the next session would be the last.

## X. TERMINATION AND FOLLOW-UP

The agenda for the final session was to discover how Molly and Dirk had managed during the intervening four weeks and to check each item on the assessment card to evaluate their progress.

The Connollys reported that they had done some more arranging in the house and Dirk's father had finally found his own apartment. They also reported that the level of stress in the household had decreased significantly and that there had been fewer arguments among the children. Dirk attributed the children's improved behavior to the fact that they were tired of suffering the consequences for failed expectations. Both Molly and Dirk claimed that they were more relaxed and didn't get as worked up over the children's misbehavior. Instead, they simply enforced whatever consequences had been previously determined. Dirk also reported that Molly no longer overexplained to the children. Molly said that she now felt confident about setting up expectations and consequences and had seen the effectiveness of doing so, both at home and at school. Both Dirk and Molly stated that they recognized that the children would continue to test them and that they felt apprehensive about the possibility of slipping back into their old habits.

Dirk expressed excitement over his daughter Melanie's coming to visit in the summer. He spoke about how he had to reestablish a relationship with her and how he had to be careful not to spoil her. The Connollys had already discussed how they were going to handle Melanie when she was with them and had mutually agreed that she would have to abide by all the house rules, just as the other children did.

Dirk remarked that he and Molly now knew what to do when a problem arose, even though they realized that a situation might not change overnight. He added that things were at their worst whenever he and Molly stopped communicating. Previously, they had assumed that problems would just take care of themselves. They now realized that they had to discuss a situation and make a plan for its solution.

Their view of Jimmy had also changed. Instead of labeling him "the rotten kid" or "the monster of the family," they understood that he was really the most sensitive and perceptive of the children. Insightfully, Dirk declared that Jimmy was "a gauge of where we are at." He added that, when things were not good between Molly and him, Jimmy was at his worst. They were cognizant that Jimmy's behavior was not spiteful or deliberate but that he was picking up on his parents' emotions and behavior and acting out accordingly. Furthermore, they had become aware that each child had a different way of dealing with stress and that Jimmy's way happened to be throwing a tantrum.

The therapists then brought up the issue of communication. They told the couple that they had noticed that they were now more responsible for their individual communication, each speaking for himself or herself and each owning his or her own thoughts and feelings. Dirk complimented Molly on her improved openness. Molly commented that she now felt more in touch with the children, more in touch with Dirk, and more able to express herself. Dirk confessed that he used to ignore Molly and that now he would ask her how she was doing and really listen to her response. Molly stated that she did the same. The therapists noticed that the couple's tendency to make assumptions had decreased considerably. In fact, Molly had initiated some perception checks right within the session.

The therapists continued to note that Dirk did not take compliments well. While they were giving feedback about all the improvements that the couple had made, Dirk was disclosing his shortcomings. He said that he still had difficulty giving positive reinforcement to the children. He claimed that while Molly was caring and nurturing he was like his father—very critical. However, he believed that he had become more sensitive about being critical of the children. Molly countered that she saw Dirk as very good with the children and that he was harder on himself than on anyone else. The therapists mentioned that, now that Dirk was feeling and acting like an equal parent, perhaps he could "loosen up a bit." He replied that the children knew how uptight he could be and that they were therefore able to push his buttons.

As the session drew to a close, the Connollys pursued the issue that had been raised in the previous session, that of Dirk's leaving the family. Dirk said that he had not realized how much this revelation would scare Molly. He then told her that, even though he sometimes felt like running away, he wouldn't do it. Molly stated that, even though they had chosen to stay together, she viewed their independence from one another as healthy. They both expressed mutual trust in each other, and Dirk said that he felt secure in the relationship.

At that point the therapists summarized all the changes that the couple had made since beginning therapy. Molly expressed a fear of backsliding and seemed to have some anxiety about terminating. The therapists reinforced the fact that the two had the tools they needed to solve their own problems. But they also left the door open, inviting Dirk and Molly to call if they felt they wanted to have a follow-up session.

In closing, the therapists highlighted how motivated the couple had been, how quickly the two had absorbed the concepts of the model, and how hard they had worked to change. They were then wished good luck and sent on their way.

The Connollys were contacted by the supervisor approximately eight months after termination. The family had maintained the changes initially made in therapy and had established a satisfying problem-solving process. Normal "kid" problems were being handled in a timely fashion, and the parents reported enjoyable times together with the children. Stress no longer appeared to be an unmanageable issue. The entire family was looking forward to Dirk's graduation from college in two months. They were also anticipating his employment as a teacher. The increase in income would allow them to move to a larger apartment and eventually to own their own home. The family was effectively managing present-day problems and optimistically planning for the future. The supervisor complimented Molly on the family's progress and offered future assistance if needed. The family never called back.

## XI. THERAPIST REACTION AND EVALUATION

This case was a textbook example of the efficient use of the Integrative Model. The Connollys were a young, chaotic family with additional environmental stressors. The adults had a committed relationship after difficult first marriages, but their new marriage was threatened by daily incidents at home, work, and school that appeared to them to be unmanageable. They were living in a situation that was causing high anxiety and that seemed to present few alternatives for change.

The therapeutic team immediately recognized the care the two had for each other and their desire for change. The team continually noted the family's commitment to counseling and motivation to complete homework assignments. By normalizing their situation and giving the adults new tools to organize and manage the family, the therapists created an optimistic environment. As the couple very quickly began to implement the mutual goals listed on the assessment cards, the two experienced relief and success. Once the child-management issue was under control, the Connollys were able to address their own personal concerns and to deal with new crises (Amanda's molestation, the presence of Dirk's father) as they arose. By the later sessions, the family was problem solving on its own, and the therapists' role became one of support.

The nine sessions represent a typical length of time in the model. This is the way that the Integrative Model was designed to work, as it does in a majority of cases. A top rating of 5 seemed to be appropriate for this case.

### *Rating*

X

| *1* | *2* | *3* | *4* | *5* |
|---|---|---|---|---|
| no goals attained 0% | few goals attained 25% | half of goals attained 50% | most goals attained 75% | all goals attained 100% |

# CHAPTER 2

# The Overwhelmed Mother: Single-Parent Family

## WILLIAM M. WALSH

Co-therapists: Patricia Bywalec
Bernadette Veeneman
Supervisors: Paul Farina
William M. Walsh

## I. IDENTIFYING DATA

The Nelsons are a single-parent family. Debra is a thirty-nine-year-old divorced mother of two boys: Ethan, age nine; and Philip, age six. The boys' father, Edward, age thirty-seven, lives in another part of the country. He has periodic telephone contact and twice a year visits with the boys. He is an electrical engineer who is currently unemployed. Debra receives sporadic child-support payments from her ex-husband.

Debra is employed full-time as an administrative secretary for a local government agency. She and the boys live in an old house in a middle-class suburban area of a midwestern city. They plan to move soon to an apartment in the same area because of escalating housing costs. Ethan is a third-grade student in a gifted education program at a local public

52

elementary school, and Philip is a first-grade student at the same school. Edward and Debra have been divorced for five years, and neither has remarried. Debra is currently dating Frank, a mental health therapist in her community.

## II. INTRODUCTORY MATERIAL

Mrs. Nelson called for a counseling appointment after discussing her situation with Frank. He suggested that she consider family therapy with the University clinic, since he had a developing personal relationship with her and the boys. On the telephone she shared her concerns about her sons. She described constant sibling tension and arguing, because Ethan continually provoked and manipulated Philip. Ethan also displayed an "extraordinary degree" of irresponsibility at home and to a "lesser extent" at school. Mrs. Nelson said she had "mother burnout" and that there was a lack of play and enjoyment between mother and children. "It's all work," she said with a sigh. There was also ongoing financial stress caused by her ex-husband's emotional instability and irresponsibility according to Debra. Edward was in therapy in his community, and reportedly attended A.A. meetings on a regular basis. Debra also described him as a compulsive runner. During their marriage her ex-husband was physically abusive to her on occasion. Ethan had witnessed several of those incidents. Debra characterized their years together as a "violent marriage." She believed that her boys were angry with their father and that this rage triggered acting-out and irresponsible behavior in Ethan. Although very bright and gifted academically, Ethan was forgetful of most things at home and in school.

All of this introductory material was obtained on the telephone by the clinic supervisor. Mrs. Nelson was very verbal and articulate, and she wished to say as much as possible in a short period of time.

## III. INFORMATION GATHERING (SESSIONS 1 AND 2)

Debra Nelson presented herself at the first session as a bright, articulate, soft-spoken, well-educated woman. Both boys were also present and sat quietly in separate chairs. The therapists began the session by describing the treatment situation, their therapeutic backgrounds, and their general goals for the first three sessions. They explained that she would receive a family assessment card in the third session that would describe the therapists' goals for the remainder of therapy. These goals would be discussed with her and mutually agreed upon. She would then be asked to commit to regular therapeutic contacts. Mrs. Nelson was then asked to make a commitment for three sessions and to sign therapeutic consent forms. One of the therapists mentioned that much of the work in therapy would be done outside of the sessions and that homework assignments for all would be a part of the process. Debra immediately responded in the affirmative and said that she knew change was a continual process.

The therapists asked Debra to review her current situation and relevant parts of her past. She briefly related the same information that was discussed on the telephone and talked about the loss of her house and the impending move to an apartment. The forced sale of the home was precipitated by the nonpayment of support by her ex-husband. Ethan was asked about his feelings toward the move, and he talked about several new features in the apartment that he liked. Philip was also encouraged to express his feelings about the move, and he added several items to Ethan's list. Debra said that they were all looking forward to the new living situation, and the boys could now walk to the same school. Additionally, living expenses would be considerably less in the apartment, and Debra felt that this would lower the stress in the family.

The therapists shifted the focus of the session and asked Debra to discuss her marriage. Debra thoughtfully described Edward's family background. Both of his parents were high-achieving professionals, and his older sister was chronically mentally ill. Debra said she liked all of them. "Honestly, they are all nice people." Edward, she said, had always been compulsive, and his therapists have told her that he was an alcoholic and a narcissistic personality. She continued to be frequently confused by his discontinuous or different versions of events that she saw in a different order. After therapists' promptings Debra described several conflicts that resulted in violence. The explosions had become progressively worse and had taken on a paranoidlike flavor. Co-workers of Edward had described similar behavior to her. He was frequently absent, and she never knew what moods he would display when he did come home. She had not been working at the time and felt she had low self-esteem. She described herself as being a confused and depressed mother who was isolated and lonely during this time. For three years Ethan had witnessed his father's "bizarre" behavior. Edward had left the home when Philip was an infant. Debra believed that he has not affected as directly as Ethan. Debra and Edward have been divorced for five years.

The therapists asked Ethan about the time when his Dad was home. Through a series of questions Ethan said he had been frightened but felt good now that Dad was gone. Both boys saw their father twice a year for several days. He also telephoned them biweekly. Ethan was particularly interested in the computer programs that his father gave him, and Philip liked the books that "Daddy gives me." The therapists then talked to both boys about their fights together. Much time was spent engaging them and clarifying aspects of their relationship. Debra felt that the boys' difficult relationship was the crux of the problem. Ethan frequently yelled at Philip when Debra was home, thereby involving her in their conflicts. The therapists asked for examples, and Debra and Ethan related several. Debra said that Ethan may have become the "scapegoat" in the family, but that she didn't want this to happen. At school Ethan was a gifted student, but he "forgets everything." Homework was particularly difficult, but Ethan said it was getting better. The forgetfulness occurred at home also. Mornings were particularly chaotic and conflictual. Ethan also forgot to use his inhaler and to take his medication to prevent asthma attacks. This had often resulted in rushed trips to the hospital emergency room. Both boys talked about their friends and playtime outside of home and school.

Debra said that the primary areas of concern for her were the fighting, the provoking behavior, the need for constant involvement, and the continual checking on Ethan so that he didn't forget important tasks. "He literally forgets what he is supposed to do from point A to point B," she said. This was particularly serious when it involved his medication. She felt constantly involved with him and said, "It is so much work. . . . There is little joy in this family now." Debra had no family in the area, so she felt she had no relief from family responsibilities. She had not dated much since the divorce, but she was now involved with a man who helped her with the boys whenever he was present. However, their contact was sporadic. The constant checking and reminding of Ethan had worn her out. She was frequently angry with him for his forgetfulness, and this anger colored the relationship among the three of them.

Ethan has been seeing a school counselor weekly for three years. Apparently, the sessions have involved play therapy and discussions of school activities and behaviors. Attention has focused on his "unresolved rage" and his constant forgetfulness, according to Debra. She gave her permission for the therapists to talk with the school counselor.

As the session progressed, the therapists found it easier to engage the boys, who became more spontaneous in discussing situations at home and at school. Ethan was particularly good with a computer, which reminded Debra of his father. Ethan also looked like his Dad and "deals with life like his father does." Philip was more like her, she believed. After a question by the therapist, Debra said that the similarity between

Ethan and his father was a concern for her. The therapist asked Debra about other concerns. She said that Philip needed to find his niche in the family, and Ethan needed to be less explosive.

At the end of the first session, all family members were asked to think about what they wanted to change in the family. Debra agreed to make a list of these desired changes after consulting the boys. The session ended with therapists' compliments to the family members about their openness and apparent willingness to change.

The second session, one week later, started with a discussion of the homework. All three family members had written lists of changes that each wanted in the family. The therapists asked them to present their lists, and the family decided that Philip would start. He read his list, which involved six requests of Ethan to change his behavior toward Philip. Ethan was second with his list of four changes, most of which involved his mother's behaving differently toward him. Debra presented her list last. The six points on her list were:

1. Ethan to stop teasing and manipulating Philip.
2. Both boys to solve their conflicts and lessen their requests for her involvement.
3. Ethan to become less forgetful at home and school.
4. Both children to become more responsible for cleaning their own clutter.
5. All of them to identify times when they could have fun together.
6. To work out a consistent financial arrangement with her ex-husband.

The therapists complimented all of the family members on their motivation in preparing the lists. This appeared to be a very positive sign that the family was ready to change and also to do the hard work to accomplish that.

The therapist then requested more information about Debra's male friend, Frank. Debra said that she was fearful of a further commitment at this time but saw positive aspects in her involvement with him. He was recently divorced and was somewhat tentative about their relationship, also. She said he was "integral to the kids," and that the boys liked him to be around. Much time was spent with all three discussing their feelings about Debra's friend and their wishes for his future involvement in the family.

Debra and Frank have been dating for one year, and he has been more involved with the boys in the last six months. He was raised in an adult family, and he tended to be more adultlike with the kids. She was "in her head most of the time" and not very playful, either. She wanted both of them to be more playful with the children. He has a teenage daughter and a three-year-old daughter from his first marriage. He has a good relationship with both of them. Through his own therapy and discussions with Debra in the past year, he has become more responsive with the boys. The family members then spent time discussing their relationship with Frank. All agreed that they were now much closer to him than when he first started dating Debra.

The therapists then turned the focus to a further discussion of Edward's continuing role in the family. About once a month he sent a cassette of children's stories that he had recorded for the boys. Debra felt that he had a sense of resonsibility for the boys but that he was more connected to Ethan than to Philip.

Debra then continued her discussion of her relationship with Edward. Their separation and divorce had been a mutual decision, and Edward shortly thereafter moved to another part of the country. Debra frequently felt alone and overwhelmed by her parental responsibilities. She returned to work a year after the separation. Divorce-adjustment groups and her return to work helped her to lower her anxiety and to develop better coping skills with the boys.

The therapists asked about her courtship with Edward. Much time was spent describing an "intensely romantic relationship." However, when they had conflicts she blamed herself. This continued into their marriage and throughout a brief marital-counseling process. Since the divorce she has resolved her guilt through personal counseling, and now feels that most of the problems were a result of Edward's "insane behavior." Even though the initial adjustment to single-parenthood was "extremely difficult," she believed it was necessary for her survival and that of her sons.

Debra talked about her family of origin and her childhood. Her parents were conflictual and emotionally separate. They were older when she was born, and she frequently thought that she was adopted. Debra slept with her mother for many years, and both usually ate meals separate from her father. Her mother now lived alone, since her father died five years ago. She was not sure how the experience of a dysfunctional family contributed to her own difficulties, but she felt her inexperience in healthy relationships left her unprepared for marriage.

The therapists then inquired about her specific expectations for both boys. She stated that they have discussed house rules and how people should behave toward one another, but the rules were rarely followed. She did not have a list of expectations, nor were there "punishments" for noncompliance. Debra said that one set of rules that was rarely followed involved Ethan's opening the house door after school, locking the door, turning up the heat in the house, and then calling his mother. He often forgot to lock the door or turn up the heat. She was very concerned about this and nagged him daily. Ethan began to cry in the session as his mother described the situation. He said he felt badly when he forgot and his mom got mad at him. The family dialogued briefly about this, and the therapists complimented the family members about their caring, support, and good communication skills.

The therapist asked Debra about her view of the world. Debra unhesitatingly said that her view was negative and that she believed that most of life is a struggle. "Nothing comes easy," she said, "and much work is needed to succeed at anything. This involves relationships, too." She saw herself as untrusting and a firm believer in "Murphy's Law." (What can go wrong will go wrong).

Toward the end of the session the therapists told Ethan that they had talked to his school counselor and that she told them how well he was doing in counseling. They then asked the family to discuss among themselves in the session a fun thing to do in the next week. All of them shared ideas, and they decided to go to a museum or to the zoo, depending on the weather. The therapists then assigned this activity for homework.

# IV. INTEGRATIVE EVALUATION

**Structure:**

**Roles:**

**Communication/Perception:**

**Themes:**

**Individual Personality Dynamics:**

## V. FAMILY ASSESSMENT CARD

The assessment of your family's strengths and weaknesses is based on observation and clinical evaluation by your therapists in consultation with the supervisory staff.

The assessment will provide important information for your family. A commitment by each family member to work on mutually agreed-upon goals both in the sessions and at home between the sessions will maximize the value of this assessment. Work on each of the goals will help your family to function more effectively and help each family member to change and grow.

_____

_____

_____

_____

_____

_____

_____

_____

_____

_____

_____

_____

_____

_____

_____

_____

_____

# VI. COMPLETED INTEGRATIVE EVALUATION

**Structure:**
Mother is overinvolved in the sibling subunit; Debra's ex-husband invades Debra's adult unit as well as her daily parenting activities; good relationship between Debra and Frank; Frank is not included in the parental subunit

**Roles:**
*Expectations:* Not clear, not specific
*Consequences:* Not clear, not specific, not appropriate
*Follow-Through:* Inconsistent for both boys

**Communication/Perception:**
*Communication:* Conflictual among all family members; boys use arguing and blaming
*Perception:* Ethan does not listen to Mother

**Themes:**
Anxiety and stress related to single-parent lifestyle; parenting difficulties; negative view of life; lack of adult relationships; conflictual postdivorce situation

**Individual Personality Dynamics:**
*Debra:* Low energy; negative view of the world; cognitively oriented; low affective awareness
*Edward:* Paranoid; narcissistic personality; conflictual; violent
*Frank:* Cognitively oriented; low affective awareness

## VII. COMPLETED FAMILY ASSESSMENT CARD

> The assessment of your family's strengths and weaknesses is based on observation and clinical evaluation by your therapists in consultation with the supervisory staff.
>
> The assessment will provide important information for your family. A commitment by each family member to work on mutually agreed-upon goals both in the sessions and at home between the sessions will maximize the value of this assessment. Work on each of the goals will help your family to function more effectively and help each family member to change and grow.
>
> 1. Clear and age-appropriate expectations, consequences, and follow-through need to be set down for both boys.
> 2. Debra needs to develop nourishing adult relationships.
> 3. Debra needs to let her sons work out their differences without interfering.
> 4. Ethan and Philip need to tell each other what they need from one another.
> 5. The family needs to build "fun time" into its schedule each week.
> 6. Debra needs to explore in which situations her children remind her of her ex-husband.
> 7. Debra needs to be aware of her ex-husband's invasion into her adult and parental subunits.

## VIII. ASSESSMENT (SESSION 3)

Session three began with a review of the previous week's homework assignment. Debra reported that they had spent Sunday in a museum and then went for a long walk in a large park. The boys enthusiastically related their experiences to the therapists. When they arrived back home, Ethan suggested that they all draw pictures of their experiences that day. Debra brought these pictures to the session to show the therapists. The discussion and the picture show-and-tell resulted in much laughter among the therapists and all family members.

The therapists then introduced the assessment card and distributed one to Debra and one to the boys. The boys were asked to follow along as best they could. After the review of the card all of them would decide how the family wanted to proceed with therapy. The therapists began with goal one and explained to Debra the need for specific expectations for each child that would be appropriate for his age. The situation of clearing the dinner dishes from the table and washing them was used as an example of a clear, specific expectation. It was also pointed out to Debra that this would begin to relieve her of some of the responsibility for home care. She was further encouraged to develop a list of specific expectations for each boy and a corresponding list of consequences. Some of these consequences could be natural, while others would have to be developed by the three of them. Debra readily agreed to this process. The therapists commented that they would like to see the lists in the future and perhaps would have suggestions for modifications and additions. Debra again responded affirmatively and said that she would probably need some guidance.

Goal two involved the development of nourishing adult relationships or activities for Debra. The therapists commented that this might not involve another male relationship but would give her interests outside of work and home. Debra immediately identified several activities that she would like to do, including physical recreation at the local park district and an organized reading club. She said that this had been low on her priority list and probably shouldn't be in the future. The therapists pointed out that another aspect of this goal would involve her adult relationship with Frank as separate from her relationship with the children. Debra understood that this time in adult relationships should not involve parenting discussions or activities. She said that the fact that this was number two on the list meant she couldn't ignore it as she had in the past.

The therapists introduced goal three as a need of the sibling subunit. The boys needed to have the freedom to resolve their own problems without Debra's interference. Debra said she would need help with this from the therapists since her tolerance level was low. The therapists suggested that Debra's withdrawal of interference could be aided by setting clear, realistic expectations and consequences, as stated in goal one. Debra saw the usefulness of that, and she was anxious to begin.

Goal four also involved the sibling subunit. The therapists told the boys that they would teach them how to talk and listen to each other better. Debra would become a part of this teaching process rather than an arbitrator of disputes. Goal five was dependent on a new organization of tasks so that time was available for family pleasure rather than as a last priority. Debra said that as the boys took over more responsibilities, she would not feel as exhausted and would enjoy their time together. The therapists used the recent museum trip as an example of an activity that could be planned on a weekly basis. The therapists reinforced Debra's desire to free up energy for the boys.

The therapists asked Debra to think of examples for goal six. She immediately focused on the physical similarities between Edward and Ethan and between her and Philip. She also noted that Ethan's explosiveness and irresponsibility were similar to Edward's. Philip, on the other hand, was more like Debra in being the responsible one who took care of things for Ethan. The therapists told Debra that they would focus on this goal throughout the remaining sessions. Debra's task now was to become more aware of these comparisons on a daily basis.

The final goal related to the continuing involvement of Edward in Debra's adult relationships by his repeated questions and comments about her friends. The therapists related several examples from past sessions that Debra had shared with them, and Debra identified several more examples of Edward's invasion into her parenting role. She had tried to ignore these intrusions, but she agreed with the therapists that she needed to develop a clearer boundary around the family unit. She wanted to increase the reliability of Edward's financial contributions without also accepting his blame and advice.

The therapists stated that they would work with her in the ensuing sessions to accomplish the goals on the assessment card. Some work would be done in the sessions, and other assignments would be for homework. They asked for questions and comments from the family. Debra said that for some ''unknown reason'' in the last week Ethan had been remembering to do what was expected of him. He had been taking his medication and turning up the heat. It was evident to the therapists that system changes had already begun to occur without apparent conscious awareness by family members. The therapists encouraged Debra to positively connote these changes as they happened.

At the end of the session homework was assigned that involved the development of expectations and consequences by Debra (goal one). The boys were to begin resolving their differences without Mom (goal three). They all agreed to the homework and said that Mom would be on vacation regarding goal three. The next session was scheduled for the following week.

# IX. SUBSEQUENT SESSIONS

One week later, session four began with Debra's describing the development of the list of expectations and consequences. She had involved the boys in discussions during the week, and they had mutually agreed on five daily tasks each and several more that were to be done weekly. The therapists commented on each and clarified specifics. Debra noted these suggestions on her list. The therapists reinforced the need for ongoing negotiations among the three. Debra preferred to emphasize positive consequences while using negative natural consequences only when appropriate. This was a surprise to the therapeutic team, given Debra's negative outlook on life. She had been reevaluating her world view and wanted to become a more positive person. The therapists again positively connoted the family's efforts.

Debra commented that the noise level had decreased in the home. The boys were arguing less, and she was trying to give them less negative attention. The therapist mentioned that the time they now spent together was more positive, and that the boys needed fewer negative attention-getting behaviors to involve her. Sundays were now their time together. They called it their "vacation day."

Debra suggested that they begin using charts, and the boys wanted to help design them. Ethan was more spontaneously vocal in this session, and Philip began to pick up on his lead. Throughout the session, the therapists told the boys that their increase in responsible behavior allowed the whole family to spend more fun time together. The boys in turn suggested more activities to do together.

The therapists asked the boys how they had done with their homework of resolving their differences. Ethan said that whenever he teased his brother, Philip said he wouldn't get involved. Ethan said that "it just stopped." The therapists had the boys and Debra role-play two situations where Ethan teased Philip, and they both tried to involve Mom. When she stayed removed (clear boundary), they stopped trying to involve her. Debra observed the interactions in the session and identified places where she could have become involved in their conflicts. The boys were encouraged by the therapists to continue solving their problems in the next week, because Mom had another week off.

The therapists then shifted the focus of the session to Debra's adult relationships. She said that she had been thinking about various activities but had not chosen anything yet. She didn't want "mindless activities." The therapists commented that anything that nourished her would be appropriate. They said that they didn't want her to lose sight of the need to replenish herself. Debra also briefly talked about Frank and their recent relationship issues. She said that she thought she loved him, but she wondered about her fear of intimacy. She asked herself if she was running away from intimacy. She wanted to take some "relationship risks" but wondered if she was ready. The therapist encouraged her to stretch her boundaries about relationships, asked her what it would take to lighten up her relationship with Frank. "Right now", she said, "it feels so heavy." Debra said that perhaps she didn't need long-term answers now, even though that was what she had always wanted.

Since their move to the apartment was to occur the following week, the therapists suggested that her search for long-term answers in her adult relationship be put on hold. They encouraged her to focus on fun with Frank in the near future. They would review the relationship in the next session. The therapists reviewed again the homework for the boys and encouraged Debra to continue working on expectations and consequences. They suggested that the next session be scheduled for two weeks in order for the family members to accomplish their homework and settle in the new apartment. The family agreed to this schedule.

Two weeks later all family members attended the fifth session. The therapists opened the session by reviewing the homework. Debra said that the family had been very occupied by the move to the apartment. She felt that they had lost touch with their assignments, and that the boys had regressed somewhat in their behavior.

The therapists reiterated the homework assignments and normalized the stress that had resulted from the move. The family members proceeded to discuss among themselves what had happened during the past two weeks and what they now wanted to do. As the discussion continued it became clear that many of the changes had been maintained despite Debra's negative feelings. Debra had explored options for herself regarding adult activities, and she had narrowed her choices to three that she would try in the next week. The boys had continued to resolve their difficulties, and they had involved their Mom less in their conflicts. Debra said that there was one instance of fighting in which she was forced to intervene, and she found out that the boys were not really fighting, but that they were playing a trick on her. The result was spontaneous laughter that surprised her. This had rarely happened in the past. As she reflected in the session, Debra realized that her feelings were more a result of her negative mind-set and the stress of the move than any actual regression. The boys then related several more incidents of spontaneous fun that they had initiated. The therapists commented that the planned fun times did not happen, but that spontaneous fun took place instead. Debra said that her uptight person was freed up without her knowing it.

Debra focused on the stress she had experienced because of the move and legal difficulties with the sale of the house. She appeared to be tired and frustrated. Frank had helped her with unpacking and chores, and Debra said that she had never seen that side of him. The therapists commented on her new insight into Frank's behavior and the degree of caring that he exhibited. Debra felt that she had not given him enough credit for this. The therapists focused on the significance of the move as a new chapter in their family life. Debra reflected on her feelings of grief at leaving but said the new place was more hospitable for them. She said, "I am going from the dark into the light."

As the session progressed, Debra began responding more positively and laughed on several occasions. She seemed to gain energy from the positive comments of the therapists and began to plan her own homework for the next two weeks. She planned to stay uninvolved with the sibling conflicts, to develop the expectation-and-consequence charts, and to start the adult activities. The session closed with Debra's verbally recommiting herself to the therapeutic goals and reflecting on Frank's caring attitude. The therapists noted the change in her attitude from negative to positive as the session had progressed. They stated that her attitude colored her view of the family and its behavior.

The sixth session began two weeks later with the therapists reviewing the move and checking on the homework assignments. Debra reported that she had completed the chart of expectations and consequences and had brought it to the session. She said that the boys were completing all of their tasks, and that she was keeping track on the chart. The boys were also checking the chart to monitor their progress. The therapists then asked the boys if they were resolving their conflicts and helping Mom to stay disengaged. They felt that this was occurring most of the time. Debra agreed, but she identified several incidents where she was drawn into the conflict. They all agreed that they needed more work on this goal.

The therapists then asked the boys to draw several pictures of what they wanted from each other. They sat at a table in the therapy room that was removed from the seating arrangement. This allowed Debra and the therapists to talk in private. In the ensuing discussion, the therapists discovered that many of Debra's interventions were appropriate as a control mechanism for the boys. They then set new expectations for the boys that involved appropriate play activities in an apartment building.

The remainder of the session was devoted to discussions of the other goals on the assessment card. All family members were getting more involved in extrafamilial activities. Debra had joined a community theater production, a reading club, and a dance class. Philip and Ethan had begun a karate class, and Ethan was in a boys choir. This had given them all time away from each other, and it had also required the boys to become more responsible for their class preparation and attendance. Debra also had begun to limit Edward's access to her personal adult relationships and to clarify his parental role. She talked to him several times about these issues, and he appeared to be moderately accepting of her wishes. He had also become occupied with settling into a new job and a new community. Debra went on to discuss her continuing relationship with Frank and her fear of sexual closeness. She had begun to talk with him about her fear of intimacy and how this affected their relationship. The therapists closed the session by reinforcing Debra's need to continue these dialogues as well as to continue working on the other therapeutic goals. The therapists and Debra also decided that if the family continued to change at the same rate, the next session would be the final one. The therapeutic team had discussed this possibility for several weeks, and the family seemed ready to consider it also.

## X. TERMINATION AND FOLLOW-UP

Three weeks later the therapists began the final session by reviewing all of the major goals on the assessment card. They used examples from the past sessions to illustrate the changes that had occurred in the family. The boys became involved in the discussion of expectations, and Ethan suggested that they develop more charts, called "Great Expectations II" and "Great Expectations III." Throughout the discussion it was evident to the therapists that the family was very involved in structuring expectations and consequences, and that the boys were responding well to the feedback from the chart. The use of natural consequences was becoming easier for Debra.

The therapist then asked Debra to review her feelings about the boys' relationship and her role in it. She related that she still jumped in when the conflict escalated to an intolerable level. The therapist suggested that Debra limit the time of a conflict and then apply an appropriate consequence. Once the consequence had been applied, she would then disengage. Debra felt that this was a good alternative that gave her control yet didn't get her "hooked" by the boys. The therapists normalized her difficulties by stating that modifications in the application of the goals were common as therapy progressed. Debra also expressed concern about her unfamiliarity with the normal behavior of children, since she was an only child without much contact with extended family. The therapists stated that they were aware of that situation and were, therefore, referring her to an ongoing parenting class in her community. They encouraged her to attend, stating that it would be an appropriate extension of the family counseling process.

The individual activities for each family member were continuing. Debra was enjoying her time away from the family as an adult, which she felt was energizing. Ethan enjoyed his activities and was following through responsibly each week preparing for the next choir practice and karate lesson. Philip was resisting the work and practice involved in the karate class. Debra, however, felt he should participate a short while longer until the class was over. She believed that this would teach him the responsibility of continuing an activity to completion. The therapists reinforced Debra's attitude.

The therapists shifted the focus to Edward's continued involvement with the boys as a parent. Debra had structured him out of the adult unit and felt that he should have minimal involvement in parenting, since he had chosen to move across the country. For five years he had been a parent at a distance and would probably remain that way. However, she felt his intrusions were decreasing and were at an acceptable level. In the past week, Debra had discussed her decisions with Edward's parents, and they were supportive of her. The new job had involved him in other activities, which gave him less energy to get involved in her life.

The therapists then reviewed her continuing relationship with Frank, which occupied a significant portion of the session. She now felt more comfortable talking to him about intimacy and sex. They also had their "wine and cheese" time, which was strictly adult time. The therapists talked to her about different communication strategies to use in her discussions with him, including the use of "I" statements and perception checks. Debra said that deepening this relationship had become a priority for her. She was also beginning to develop female friends. She had met several women in her theater group and her dance class, and she was enjoying spending time with them. She said that she had become "more aware of how emotionally constricted men are, and how different it is talking to a woman." The therapists encouraged her openness to new relationships and said that she was accomplishing goal two. The therapists also emphasized the need to continue building in family "fun time" together. Debra said that she wanted to do this both with the boys and with Frank.

The therapists continued to reinforce all of the changes that had occurred in the family and stated that all seven goals on the assessment card had been accomplished. Debra verbalized that she needed to continue growing in all of the areas. The therapists reinforced her by saying that she now had the tools to make that happen.

The session ended with the therapists reviewing the assessment card again for the boys. A follow-up telephone contact was arranged for approximately six months from the final session. The therapists closed the session by complimenting the family members for their motivation and hard work.

## XI. THERAPIST REACTION AND EVALUATION

Approximately five months later, Debra Nelson was contacted by telephone by one of the supervisors. She reported that she was pleased with the way that her life was running, and that she had no major concerns. She was working at the same position, and she said that she received considerable satisfaction from her work and the increasing responsibilities that it entailed. Frank was still a part of her life, but they had not yet decided on a permanent commitment. She was not seeing anyone else. Debra now had several "girlfriends" whom she saw on an irregular basis. She was also continuing with other extrafamilial activities. Her involvement with the theater group was seasonal, but her book club met bi-weekly and her dance class twice a week. The boys, she said, were the "least of her worries." She still maintained a list of expectations and consequences for them, but this now seemed routine. Both boys were currently enrolled in a park district summer day camp, and Ethan was in a choir. Philip was not involved in any other activities. Both had done well in school, and Ethan's forgetfulness problem was history. Edward continued to telephone them biweekly and to send them occasional gifts. The boys were planning to spend one week with him at the end of the summer. Edward's inconsistent support payments continued to be a problem, and Debra was not optimistic about any change in that situation. Fortunately, she said, she was less dependent on his money since their move to the apartment. She rarely spoke to him about other topics.

An offer for further counseling did not seem necessary at that time. However, Debra was encouraged to call the clinic in the future if her circumstances changed. Based on its initial and continued success with maintaining its therapeutic goals, the Nelson family was rated by the supervisors at the highest level.

*Rating*

　　　　　　　　　　　　　　　　　　　　　　　　　　　　X

| *1* | *2* | *3* | *4* | *5* |
|---|---|---|---|---|
| no goals attained 0% | few goals attained 25% | half of goals attained 50% | most goals attained 75% | all goals attained 100% |

# PART III

# Families with An Adolescent

# CHAPTER 3

# Abused and Ignored: Intact Family

## WILLIAM M. WALSH

Co-therapists: David Fredin
Theresa Bellevage
Supervisors: Dee Stay
William M. Walsh

## I. IDENTIFYING DATA

The Warren family included Don, age forty-one; his wife Jean, age thirty-nine; two daughters, Rita, age nineteen, and Lori, age sixteen; and a son, Dennis, age twelve. Another son, Gary, age twenty-three, had just moved out five months before with his girlfriend and his young daughter. Don had asked them to leave since they were not contributing any money or help in the house.

The Warrens were a lower-middle-class family. They own a two-flat apartment building in a large city. Don has been working at a tool-and-dye factory for six years, and Jean has been at her job in a large department store for eight years. Often she works a second job part-time because she feels the family needs the extra money. She often doesn't return home until very late. Don has had some recurrent medical problems and may need further surgery. He may not be able to continue working.

Rita dropped out of high school for three years and decided to return this semester. She is still finding high school difficult and has not been attending classes regularly. Lori is a sophomore and earns good grades in school. She talks of future plans to go to college. Lori and Rita are in some of the same classes in school. They both have part-time jobs in the neighborhood at fast-food restaurants. Dennis is in the sixth grade, is a year behind in school, and is having some difficulty with his studies.

## II. INTRODUCTORY MATERIAL

The Warren family came for therapy after a high school counselor suggested that Lori and her family needed help. Lori was upset with the arguing and fighting taking place in her family and had shared some of this information with the school counselor. In particular, she couldn't understand her mother's erratic behavior. A lot of hitting and slapping were also occurring at home between Lori and her sister and between Jean and both daughters.

A few days earlier there had been an argument during dinner preparation in which there was much yelling and screaming. Lori's hand was cut with a kitchen knife that Jean was using to slice tomatoes. Lori thought that her mother was waving the knife threateningly. Rita and Lori tried to take the knife out of their mother's hand. Just a few minutes before that happened, Jean had thrown a meat-tenderizing mallet at Rita, which scratched her face. Lori talked to her father, and together they encouraged the family to come in for counseling.

Don had made the initial phone call to the supervisor, who explained that he needed to have all the members of the family come to the first session.

## III. INFORMATION GATHERING (SESSIONS 1 AND 2)

At the first session the counseling procedure was explained. All sessions were to be videotaped. A supervisory team watching the sessions in another room could phone in information or additional questions for the family. In the first two sessions as much information as possible about the family would be gathered. During the third session each family member would receive as assessment card, which would be explained in detail at that time.

During the first session, the family members discussed their background and current difficulties. Both Don and Jean Warren were from coal mining towns in Kentucky. Don had come from a very poor family. They had to fetch their own water and grow vegetables in the garden for food, but he enjoyed it. He said that he felt loved even though his parents were strict. Don finished high school and worked at odd jobs around the area for two years. He then came back to his home town and began to date Jean, whom he had met a few times previously. They were soon married. Don had had polio as a child and continued to have trouble with his leg. He also had lost sight in one eye from an accident. He mentioned that he sometimes drank and that his drinking caused problems.

Jean married Don at sixteen. She never finished high school. She came from a family of ten children. She was the eldest and had to fight to go to school. When she was in her teens, her parents would go off and leave her with the children. It was her responsibility to care for them. Jean said that her parents did a lot of swearing and smacking at each other and at the children and never showed them much love. Her parents were not happy when she ran off and got married.

Lori told the therapists that she liked school and liked working at the restaurant. She wasn't sure what she wanted to be when she grew up, but she did express that she wanted to be a success, perhaps as a teacher or nurse. She was obviously upset and didn't want to say much. She said it was difficult to talk.

Rita had her head down and was slow to talk. She spoke softly and seemed very uncomfortable about being at the session. She talked about when she was a little girl and had had a few accidents. Once she was in the hospital for months recovering from being hit by a truck. Her parents said that she was frequently involved in trouble. They stated that she had often been down and very quiet, and that a year ago she had even attempted suicide. The therapists asked her how she liked being back in school. She said that it was hard getting up in the morning and getting ready on time. Also, she found school difficult and had missed several classes.

During the first two sessions Lori explained that she and her sister had many arguments but that the most heated ones were usually between her parents and the two girls. Frequently, the arguments stemmed from the girls not being home on time, their choice of friends, the dinner not being made, the kitchen not being cleaned, or the house not being straightened. Don and Jean expressed their unhappiness with the girls' behavior and didn't want them dating. They said that the girls didn't listen to them and talked back. Jean stated that she knew many parents smacked their kids but that they didn't hit back like their girls did. Both parents felt that they had caught the girls lying and therefore couldn't trust them. Jean also stated that she realized she had a temper and that she frequently disagreed with rules or disciplinary measures implemented by her husband. She reported that she would ground Rita or Lori but then could not enforce the punishment because she was not at home. She felt that her husband protected the girls during these times.

The girls stated that they thought their parents were too strict and that they had difficulty discussing any differences with them. In particular, they felt that their mother always saw things differently or changed things around. Often she would shout orders from another room, but her instructions were not clear or specific enough for the girls to follow to her liking. She was quick to criticize and never complimented her daughters. Therefore, poor communication resulted, which was followed by blaming or lecturing by Jean and Don. This was another reason Rita had periodically run away. Rita said that her mother knew this was a problem and had said that she would try to work on it.

Toward the end of the second session, Lori said that she felt her dad wasn't speaking up enough. She also told the therapists that she would like to talk to them alone when there was time.

During the sessions Jean and Don sat apart from each other and frequently interrupted and spoke for each other as well as for the children. The therapists made note of this to the family and requested that each of them ask the last person who had spoken if he or she was finished talking before that person started. It was hoped that this would stop the interrupting and improve the communication.

For homework each family member was asked to make a list of two or more things he or she would like from one another. The therapists then summarized the session and expressed appreciation for the courage and caring the family members had shown for each other by coming for counseling. They told the family members that they showed much strength and energy but that those qualities needed to be used in more nurturing ways. The family members also needed to learn to relate to each other by talking rather than by physical and emotional outbursts. The therapists informed the family that any hint of physical abuse would have to be reported to the proper authorities. The family agreed that there would be no more abuse.

# IV. INTEGRATIVE EVALUATION

**Structure:**




**Role Expectations:**




**Communication/Perception:**




**Themes:**




**Individual Personality Dynamics:**

## V. FAMILY ASSESSMENT CARD

The assessment of your family's strengths and weaknesses is based on observation and clinical evaluation by your therapists in consultation with the supervisory staff.

The assessment will provide important information for your family. A commitment by each family member to work on mutually agreed-upon goals both in the sessions and at home between the sessions will maximize the value of this assessment. Work on each of the goals will help your family to function more effectively and help each family member to change and grow.

_____

_____

_____

_____

_____

_____

_____

_____

_____

_____

_____

_____

_____

_____

# VI. COMPLETED INTEGRATIVE EVALUATION

**Structure:**
Chaotic; rigid boundary between husband and wife; conflictual between father, mother, and daughters; diffuse boundary around Rita; invasion of parental unit by daughters; mother is chidlike; lack of a parental team

**Roles:**
*Expectations:* Undefined and confused due to lack of parenting skills, lack of problem-solving skills, and lack of parental responsibility (mother)
*Consequences:* None
*Follow-Through:* None

**Communication/Perception:**
*Communication:* Inadequate and incomplete communication in parental team; lack of expression of needs and emotions, both husband and wife; blaming, yelling, lecturing, distortions, criticizing; physical abuse; interrupting
*Perception:* Poor listening, diffusing, and avoiding; defensiveness

**Themes:**
Marital dissatisfaction; lack of mutuality in parental team; lack of parenting skills; lack of trust; erratic and harsh discipline; physical and verbal abuse; Rita skipping classes and future plans; independence vs. dependence issues; Don's health concerns and alcohol problem; parents being strict about dating; lack of affection

**Individual Personality Dynamics:**
*Don:* alcohol problem, self-esteem, avoidance, denial, doesn't express needs
*Jean:* erratic behavior, angry, resentful, dishonesty, unloving, irritable, accusatory
*Rita:* depressed, dishonesty, angry, needing direction, focus on the negative
*Lori:* angry, depressed, the savior
*Dennis:* fights in school

## VII. COMPLETED FAMILY ASSESSMENT CARD

> The assessment of your family's strengths and weaknesses is based on observation and clinical evaluation by your therapists in consultation with the supervisory staff.
>
> The assessment will provide important information for your family. A commitment by each family member to work on mutually agreed-upon goals both in the sessions and at home between the sessions will maximize the value of this assessment. Work on each of the goals will help your family to function more effectively and help each family member to change and grow.
>
> 1. All family members need to improve their communications skills by practicing clear and direct statements:
>    a. Look at the person and make eye contact.
>    b. Be specific.
> 2. All family members need to improve listening skills:
>    a. Check out if the other person has finished speaking; no interruptions.
>    b. Listen to what is being said, and then decide on your response.
> 3. Jean and Don need to agree and communicate mutual expectations for the children and for each other in specific terms:
>    a. responsibilities at home.
>    b. curfew—time to arrive or call.
>    c. school and work schedules.
> 4. Jean and Don need to agree and communicate consistent, specific consequences and follow-through for the children.
> 5. The family needs to learn to problem-solve rather than use avoidance and denial.

## VIII. ASSESSMENT (SESSION 3)

During session three the assessment card was explained to the family. The therapists stressed that each member of the family should always talk to another member face to face, making eye contact. Lecturing, blaming, or shouting directions from another room was not good communication. Don Warren was surprised that lecturing was considered to be inappropriate, since he believed that he had knowledge and experience that he should transmit to the children. However, he did admit that his messages were not receiving good responses, and that he often had to repeat himself. He also mentioned another problem. When he arrived home from work, he was mentally fatigued, but everyone wanted to talk to him at the same time. The therapists explained that he should let the family members know when he was ready to talk to each of them. At this point in the conversation, the therapists noted to the group that everyone had their eyes on Don as he talked, showing that they were already making an effort at better communication.

The therapists then explained that the parents needed to be specific about their expectations for each child. When directions were given, the statements would need to be very clear, such as, "Please bring me the largest fry pan from the cabinet." Another example given was, "Please be home at 10 P.M." instead of, "You need to be home early."

During the session Don was asked to check out statements that he heard Jean make. It was pointed out to him that he didn't always understand what Jean meant and that he should ask her to repeat her statements when this happened. Jean also realized that she was not always clear or specific with her statements.

Don expressed difficulty in forming mutual expectations, follow-through, and consequences with Jean in regard to the children. The therapists emphasized the importance of this process. They reminded Don that he had given a very good example earlier in the session. Don and Jean had allowed Gary and his girlfriend to move into their house when Gary didn't have a job. Eventually Gary got a job, and the baby arrived. However, Gary wasn't contributing to the upkeep of the family, and both Gary and his girlfriend were creating a chaotic situation. Don and Jean had given him an ultimatum to either move out or pay some rent and help with repairs that were needed. When his behavior didn't change, Don told him to leave. The therapists stated that this was a good example of a clear expectation, follow-through, and consequence.

Throughout this session, the therapists made sure to be supportive of Jean Warren, because they knew she had been uncomfortable and that she played an important part in the things that happened at home. She told the therapists that she had mentioned to a friend that she was going to therapy, and that she was encouraged by the positive changes in the family. The therapists, in turn, complimented the family members for their openness and their willingness to look at themselves.

## IX. SUBSEQUENT SESSIONS

During the fourth and fifth sessions, the intent of the therapists was to demonstrate the usefulness of the concept of family subunits and to encourage sufficient privacy to allow subunit members to express their individual feelings. Therefore the format was changed so that the first ten minutes of each session was devoted to the entire family. The balance of the time was divided into two sessions. The parents met alone for the first half, and the children met alone for the second half. Both groups were told that the information was confidential unless they wanted certain facts brought up later when the entire family met.

During these sessions Jean related that she had had two nervous breakdowns for which she had been hospitalized. Furthermore, on several occasions she had left the family for months at a time to live with friends. Jean explained that she often became depressed and could not be around children. During these periods of Jean's absence, Don had difficulty getting good help to run the household. However, whenever things would begin to go smoothly, Jean would reappear. Don would always take her back. He felt that the children had a real sense of insecurity as a result of Jean's absences. Don said that Jean continued to leave now and that didn't know whether she was shopping or working. Jean's explanations were, to him, vague, defensive, and hard to understand. Don spoke of trust between two people. The therapists agreed that trust was important, because a lack of trust was divisive to a relationship.

The Warrens were asked what the two of them could do to make the family better. However, the two found it difficult to address this question because of all the issues they had avoided for so long. They needed to be reminded to face each other and to make eye contact. They finally mentioned yelling, attitudes, and control.

When the sibling subunit met, Lori told the therapists that their mother had boyfriends but that their father would not talk about it. Everyone knew that the parents had talked of divorce at times. Rita had heard parts of conversations, which caused her mother to be angry with her. Both girls had seen their mother hanging out at a restaurant with men. The therapists empathized with Lori and the others but explained that Jean and Don had to work out their own issues. They explained that their parents were adults who had to decide what they wanted to do about the situation. The therapists then asked how the communication homework was working. The children responded that they saw some improvements at home and that they were having some fun with it.

In subsequent sessions the therapists were told that Don's whole family back home had drinking problems. Although Don admitted to drinking, he also tried to make light of it. Each family member was asked to tell Don what he looked like, how he acted, and what he said when he was drinking. Don was surprised by the information, as he had been unaware of his effect on others. He felt that, because most of his drinking was done on the weekends at home, it wasn't a problem since he just went to sleep. He didn't drive a car or get into fights, and he always went to work on Mondays. Don was told that he needed to stop drinking. He stated that he was willing to work on it. He was told that his drinking prevented him from facing his troubled relationship with Jean and that it was causing problems for his family. Additionally, he was told that the blackouts and loss of memory he experienced were creating potentially serious health problems. Don accepted these interventions and said that he was ready to seriously work on his problem. His ability to perceive the feedback from the family and therapists was evident, and his commitment to change seemed sincere.

Jean and Don discussed the possibility of divorce on several different occasions during sessions where everyone was present. Both Don and the children were able to express their feelings once the situation was brought into the open. After one heated session, Jean said that she thought she should get a divorce. But during the following session, both Jean and Don stated that they didn't want one. This change in attitude resulted from considerable time spent at home that week talking and listening to teach other. The children observed and commented on this new behavior. Furthermore, Don and Jean began sitting together in the sessions where previously one or more of the children sat between them. They continued to work on their relationship problems both at home and in therapy. They were slowly learning to be open and honest with their communication, which brought many old hurts to the surface. They worked at using clear and direct communication with no blaming. Don gradually reduced his drinking, although he did have some setbacks.

In one of the final sessions, the girls stated that they wished their mother would show some affection toward them. The therapists encouraged them to give hugs to their mother and even to ask for some to see if the request met with a good response. Jean seemed to find this topic somewhat uncomfortable, but she stated that she liked getting hugs. Therefore, at the end of all subsequent sessions, hugging behavior was modeled by the therapists, and the family followed suit.

Rita, Lori, and Dennis were interested in doing some family activities and were encouraged to discuss this possibility with their parents. They had a hard time figuring out an activity to do, but eventually it was decided to go to the zoo.

The following week Don and Jean were happy to report that they had put a schedule of work times and phone numbers on the refrigerator door, so that everyone would know one another's schedules. They had also completed a short list of expectations, follow-through, and consequences for the children, along with a list of expectations for each other. The therapists could see the parental subunit starting to work together in regard to the children. Furthermore, husband and wife were making an effort to enhance their own relationship. The children were being allowed to be children and were not interfering or protecting the parents. The children understood their parents' mutual expectations and consequences and were following through on them.

## X. TERMINATION AND FOLLOW-UP

The assessment card was reviewed during the last two sessions, along with the progress the therapists had seen. The family members still needed to work to keep it all together. However, they no longer found it necessary to use physical or verbal abuse. There was more clear and direct communication and better listening. The defensiveness in the unit had decreased dramatically. The family secrets were out in the open, and the family was beginning to build trust. They were showing their caring and strength by working together in a more positive direction. Therapists and family members agreed that a break from counseling was now appropriate. The therapists would call the family in approximately six months to review its situation. Family members were encouraged to call before that time if they wanted a session.

The family was called five months later to reengage its members in counseling. A session was scheduled for the following week, and the family was asked to bring its original assessment card. Don and Jean Warren, Lori and Dennis appeared for what was to be the final session. The parents sat together, and the children sat opposite them. The session began with a review of the original goals on the card. It was soon evident that the family had not regressed during the elapsed time and that most of the changes had been maintained. Don and Jean reported that they were talking and listening to each other and that they felt comfortable with their relationship. Don was not drinking, and Jean was coming directly home from work. They had established expectations for Lori and Dennis, and they were reasonably satisfied that these were accomplished most of the time. This was no longer a conflictual theme. The children agreed with all that their parents discussed. Lori was starting her senior year in high school and was thinking af attending a junior college the following year. She continued to work part-time after school. Dennis was still in junior high school, and his parents were satisfied with his progress. Rita was now living with a girlfriend in the city and was tentatively planning marriage in the next year. Don and Jean felt that this was all right, but they wished that she had completed high school. They had been encouraging her to work on her G.E.D. The therapists were struck by the positive way that the family members related to each other, using humor and complimentary remarks. They had spent time together on two short vacations the past summer, and all were surprised by the lack of conflict and increase in pleasure. In closing the session, the therapists reinforced the changes that had occurred and encouraged the family to continue to work together. The family left the therapy room with the now familiar round of hugs.

## XI. THERAPIST REACTION AND EVALUATION

The therapists' first priority had been to stop the physical abuse and lower the stress in the family. Don was a child of alcoholic parents, and Jean was neglected and severely punished as a child. Neither of them knew what normal behavior or discipline was, because of their family backgrounds. After building trust with the family, the therapists provided education and new parenting tools for Jean and Don. The family members were able to set reasonable expectations and consequences, to follow through in a more consistent fashion, and to learn new ways of relating to one another. To the surprise of the therapists, these changes were maintained over a five-month period.

The therapists provided examples of good communication and negotiation skills for the family. They provided a sense of humor to which the family responded. Don and Jean's marital problems were discussed, and Don was confronted about his drinking. In reviewing the case, the therapists felt that Don's problem drinking could have been discussed earlier in the process and that his involvement in Alcoholics Anonymous should have been encouraged. The supervisors disagreed with the suggestion for an earlier intervention, feeling that Don would not have been ready for that step, but agreed with the recommendation for A.A. Therapists and supervisors all agreed that Rita's school difficulties could have been addressed more fully and an alternative G.E.D program developed in counseling.

All things considered, the family did move through the therapeutic process in a reasonable amount of time and did build a problem-solving process that continued to endure. This, of course, is the major long-term goal of Integrative Family Therapy.

## *Rating*

X

| *1* | *2* | *3* | *4* | *5* |
|---|---|---|---|---|
| no goals attained 0% | few goals attained 25% | half of goals attained 50% | most goals attained 75% | all goals attained 100% |

# CHAPTER 4

# The Mother Who Became a Parent: Intact Family

## LEAH BERGEN
## WILLIAM WALSH

Therapists: Leah Bergman
Ronald Melman
Supervisors: Bernadette Veeneman
William M. Walsh

## I. IDENTIFYING DATA

Ann is a forty-nine-year-old divorcee who has been married three times. She has five children and five grandchildren. Sherry, the eldest daughter, is twenty-seven years old. She is married and has two children. Sherry lives in California. The second child is Janet, age twenty-five. She is married and has a daughter who is four. Janet lives nearby. Kevin, age twenty-four, is married and has a son who is six. Kevin and his family live in an apartment upstairs from his mother. Ann and her two other children, the twins, Alan, Jr., and Alana, age sixteen, and Alana's toddler Brian live in the apartment downstairs. Ann supports herself, the twins, and Brian by working as a clerk-typist.

**87**

## II. INTRODUCTORY MATERIAL

The family was referred for counseling by Alan's high school counselor because of the boy's truancy and an encounter with the police. At the time of the referral, Alan, Jr., had just been released from the Juvenile Home and was awaiting a court hearing. Alana had dropped out of school because of pregnancy and motherhood.

## III. INFORMATION GATHERING (SESSIONS 1 AND 2)

Attendees for the first session were Ann, Kevin, Alan, and Alana. The therapists explained the family-therapy format and conditions for therapy. The family agreed to the terms and willingly signed the consent forms for therapy and for videotaping the sessions.

Present interpersonal relationships within the family were described as volatile with much screaming and crying. Kevin related that he was very angry with Alan and with Alan's friends, whom Kevin described as school dropouts and troublemakers. He stated that they tried to harass him by play-fighting in front of him. Kevin said that he was also very angry with Alan for Alan's having become involved with the police for attempted car theft. He stated that he wanted to hurt Alan physically when he returned from the Juvenile Home. Apparently, Alan has been involved in other incidents with the police, such as jumping elevated train tracks to avoid paying a fare and attempted vandalism of a parking meter.

Alana stated that she had dropped out of school but was seeing a social worker, who came to the house once a week to help her with parenting and to encourage her to return to school. She reported that she spent her days caring for her son Brian and her sister Janet's four-year-old daughter. Alana also said that she always kept both children in the house, because she did not want the responsibility of taking Janet's daughter out of the house. During the day she socialized with her friends, who were also school dropouts and/or teenage mothers. On the weekends she liked to go dancing. Ann would then baby-sit for Brian. Ann complained, however, that Alana often did not return home until very late. Alana's initial appearance gave the therapists the impression of one very tough young lady. She wore heavy make-up, irregularly bleached and spiked hair, and very tight clothing. Most of the time she answered questions with, "I don't know."

Ann stated that Alan had been good in his first two years of high school. Trouble started when he began to hang around with high-school dropouts. He then started to smoke reefers and sniff spray paint. He had stopped sniffing the spray paint but was still smoking reefers. His latest incident with the police had occurred when he was caught in a neighbor's car with the keys in the ignition. The owner happened to come out while Alan was in the car, and a squad car happened to be driving by. So the police immediately arrested Alan and took him to the Juvenile Home. Two friends who were with Alan escaped and avoided being caught.

Following this brief description of the family's current situation, the therapists asked the family members to state what they expected from family therapy for the family and for themselves personally. Ann was also asked to provide a brief chronological history of her life by the next session.

Kevin did not attend the second session. Ann, Alan, and Alana showed up with Alana's son, Brian.

The session began with a review of Ann's marital and relationship history. Ann and the father of the three older children were married for nine years. Ann left him when Kevin was one year old. Between July, 1969, and June, 1972, Ann had a relationship with Alan Smith, Sr., who is the father of the twins. Ann left him because of his involvement with drugs and his womanizing. In January of 1973, Ann and Alan Sr., were reunited. He came back with promises to reform. He also bought furniture and other gifts for Ann and the children, who were very needy at the time. Ann decided to chance it, thinking that they could make it together. However, Alan was arrested one week later for being in possession of a pound of heroin. He was sentenced to twenty-years in prison. In September Ann married Alan even though he was in prison. She said that she was willing to wait twenty years for him because she loved him.

Four years later, in 1977, Ann met Tom. They lived together until 1981. At that time Ann divorced Alan and married Tom. Ann felt that things had gone well before she married Tom. But after the marriage, Tom became involved in parenting the children. In contrast to Ann's soft attitude toward parenting, Tom was tough, although not abusive. The children resented him. Tom and Kevin were extremely jealous of each other. Kevin was seventeen at the time, and he resented the fact that he was no longer "man of the house." The oldest daughter left home because of Tom. The twins disliked him also. By the middle of 1984, Tom moved out. Ann and Tom were divorced two years later.

In the meantime, Alan, Sr., had completed a drug rehabilitation program while in prison and had also gone back to school. Learning that Tom was no longer in the home, he began to write to Ann. By the end of 1986, Alan was released from prison and came to live with the family. He got a job, and things seemed to go smoothly for about three months. But he ended up back in prison with a six-year sentence for violating his parole and being in possession of a stolen vehicle. Apparently, he was driving what he though to be a friend's car when, in reality, it had been stolen.

Ann admitted that she had been getting high on drugs at one point in her relationship with Alan, Sr. She stated that she never used hard drugs but that Alan used acid.

It was interesting to observe that, when providing background information, all of the family members mentioned that they wanted Alan, Sr., back in the family. His repeated violations of the law did not seem to have any bearing on their view of him as "a beautiful person."

Meanwhile, Ann felt bad about herself and hoped to straighten out her life. She joined the Jehovah's Witnesses church and was baptized. But because she had cohabitated with Alan, Sr., she was in trouble with the church and was given only limited church privileges.

Ann stated that she presently viewed Alan, Jr., and Alana as not functioning. "They have gone down the drain." She was upset about Alana's getting pregnant and not finishing school and about Alan's involvement with the law.

Alana was not communicative during the session. She did not seem to have any goals for herself or for her son. She kept repeating "I don't know" throughout the session. She did say that she had signed up for G.E.D. classes.

Alan said that his goal was to finish high school and then go to a trade school to study computers. He was currently trying to gain admittance to a special program at a local college.

Ann has been going to Kevin for support in parenting. However, Alana stated that she was not going to listen to Kevin, since he was not her father. Ann said she had an agreement with Kevin that she could go to him for support in disciplining Alan and Alana.

Throughout the session, Ann did most of the talking, speaking not only for herself but also for the twins. She seemed to view Alana as a little girl, even though she admitted that she had no control over her. She also mentioned that she was concerned about Alana's friends, particularly her boyfriends. She said that the tone of the house was stressful, that there was much yelling but not much communicating. She believed that Brian was torn in his loyalty between Ann and Alana, as Alana often left the house for hours as soon as Ann came home.

The therapists asked the family about the homework assignment from the previous week. Alan responded that, in addition to his personal goal of finishing high school, he wished that he and his mother would be able to talk about problems and to better understand each other. Alana said that she did not know what her family goals were. She said that she would like to communicate better with her mother. She was unable to communicate with her father face to face, but she would like her father to know her better, because she realized that he didn't really know her. Ann stated that she would like to be able to talk to Alana, even if she didn't like everything that was happening. She still wanted to "talk it out." She also wanted to have the family united and able to communicate and trust each other. She was hopeful that Alan and Alana would be willing to go to Kevin with their problems. She was upset about all the yelling and screaming. She stated that she had not thought about her personal goals, that she was not worried about herself at this point.

At the end of the session the therapists requested that Ann return to the next session with five expectations each of Alan and Alana.

# IV. INTEGRATIVE EVALUATION

**Structure:**

**Roles:**

**Communication/Perception:**

**Themes:**

**Individual Personality Dynamics:**

## V. FAMILY ASSESSMENT CARD

The assessment of your family's strengths and weaknesses is based on observation and clinical evaluation by your therapists in consultation with the supervisory staff.

The assessment will provide important information for your family. A commitment by each family member to work on mutually agreed-upon goals both in the sessions and at home between the sessions will maximize the value of this assessment. Work on each of the goals will help your family to function more effectively and help each family member to change and grow.

_____

_____

_____

_____

_____

_____

_____

_____

_____

_____

_____

_____

_____

_____

## VI. COMPLETED INTEGRATIVE EVALUATION

**Structure:**
Shifting parental subunits due to serial marriages; Kevin in parental subunit but not accepted as parent by siblings; diffuse boundary between mother as parent and teenage children; diffuse and conflictual boundaries between the subunits of Alana and Brian and Ann and Brian

**Roles:**
*Expectations:* Shifting, due to Ann's failure to establish a stable marital relationship or a strong parental unit; lack of clear and situation-appropriate expectations for the twins
*Consequences:* None for either Alan or Alana
*Follow-Through:* None for Alan or Alana

**Communication/Perception:**
*Communication:* Ann speaks for the twins, also overtalks; all family members use yelling and crying instead of talking
*Perception:* Defensiveness—especially by the twins—restricts what is heard; Kevin not heard because of his not being accepted as a parent figure

**Themes:**
Hopelessness; drug abuse by mother, father, and son; lawlessness by father and son; lack of stability of parental subunit; idealization of incarcerated member by rest of family

**Individual Personality Dynamics:**
*Ann:* Low self-esteem, helplessness, lack of parenting skills, shifting alliances with different male figures
*Alan:* Hostile to authority; confused; drug-abuser
*Alana:* Unmotivated, depressed, poor self-image, lack of responsibility

## VII. COMPLETED FAMILY ASSESSMENT CARD

> The assessment of your family's strengths and weaknesses is based on observation and clinical evaluation by your therapists in consultation with the supervisory staff.
>
> The assessment will provide important information for your family. A commitment by each family member to work on mutually agreed-upon goals both in the sessions and at home between the sessions will maximize the value of this assessment. Work on each of the goals will help your family to function more effectively and help each family member to change and grow.
>
> 1. All members need to establish more clearly short- and long-term goals for themselves individually and for the family as a unit.
> 2. Family members need to become more aware of one another's concerns and expectations.
> 3. Each family member needs to become more aware of his or her own responsibilities within the family.
> 4. Kevin's role as a parent substitute needs to be more clearly defined.
> 5. As parent, Ann needs to establish clear expectations and consequences for the twins.
> 6. Ann needs to improve her communication with the family by avoiding overtalking and by speaking only for herself and not for her children.

## VIII. ASSESSMENT SESSION (SESSION 3)

Each member of the family, Ann, Kevin, Alan, and Alana, was given a copy of the assessment card. Ann agreed that she was weak in her role as a parent. The family discussed Kevin's involvement in parenting the twins. Ann admitted that she did not know how much she wanted his involvement in that process. The therapists talked with Ann about the importance of her defining her goals for herself and the family more clearly and setting clear expectations and consequences for the twins. It was explained to Ann that the setting of expectations and consequences and the following through with consequences when expectations were not met was a three-stage process. Communication problems within the family were also discussed. The point was made that each member of the family seemed to be going his or her own way and therefore no one was taking much responsibility for anything. The importance of each family member's setting individual as well as family goals was stressed.

For homework the therapists requested that Alan talk with his mother about what was happening to him at school and with his friends. This was to be done on a daily basis. Ann was to finish her list of five expectations each for Alan and Alana. Alana was to set plans and goals around her parenting of Brian.

## IX. SUBSEQUENT SESSIONS

Alana did not attend the next session because Brian was sick. Ann, Alan, and Kevin did attend.

The session began with the therapists questioning Alan about school. He said that he was having trouble studying because he was out of the routine. He had a lot of homework but said that he did it all at school. He was happy that he had made some new friends and was eating lunch with them. He reported that he no longer saw his other friends.

Ann stated that things were going much better at home. She said they were all talking to one another like human beings rather than yelling at each other. She also said that Alan and Alana were accepting more responsibility for getting chores done around the house, except that Alan was still not making his bed. Kevin and Alan were getting along better, and Kevin was teaching Alan how to take apart and fix a motorcycle. She and Alan were talking to each other each night for about one hour before going to sleep. Ann admitted that she had not yet established expectations for Alana concerning the role she would like her to take in parenting Brian. But she realized that she wanted Alana to take more responsibility in this area. Therefore, she was now telling Brian to "go to Mommy" whenever he came to her with things she felt Alana should be doing. Ann also stated that, now that the family was communicating better, she planned to establish some rules. She was unhappy with Alana's friends, whom she saw as loose and immoral. She felt that Alana stayed out too late, as Alana sometimes did not return home until 3:00 or 4:00 in the morning. Ann was encouraged by the therapists to set up rules, as it seemed that Alana was out of control. They also emphasized that it was important to establish rules and expectations so that everyone would know his or her role.

Homework assigned at the end of session four was as follows:

1. Ann and Alana were to work at improving the communication between them.
2. Everyone needed to work on listening to each other and decreasing the amount of yelling and overtalking.
3. Alan and Ann were to continue their daily talks.
4. Ann was to establish house rules and consequences.

Ann, Kevin, Alan, and Alana attended the next session. Ann reported that she had worked out her expectations for the family. She also reported that the house was clean and that things were going well. She stated that Alan was now making his bed and that both Alan and Alana were cleaning the house on the weekends. Alan had even mopped the floor, and Alana had been doing the dishes every day.

Ann then discussed the rules and consequences that she had established. If Alana stayed out late, she had to stay in the following night. If she stayed out late on Saturday night, she had to stay in for two days. Further, Ann would not baby-sit for Brian on Saturday. There were to be no boys in the house during the day, or Alana would not be allowed to go out on the weekend. Alan was to keep the basement clean and would be able to use it for entertaining his friends.

Ann further reported that she was no longer embarrassed to come home after work with friends. She said that Alan now waited for her to come home to check his room. Alan smiled as his mother reported this. Ann also stated that she now felt more confident in her parenting role. She wanted the twins to know that she needed Kevin's support only in times of crisis and would use him only if there were serious trouble. Alan's reaction to Kevin's role was, "He's all right." Alana stated, "He doesn't bother me. I don't have problems with him."

Ann mentioned that she was still concerned about Alana's late hours. She said that Brian often awoke in the middle of the night, wanting his mother. The therapists asked Ann and Alana to discuss this with each other. Alana seemed to admit that she knew what Ann meant by saying, "I don't know what to say." When asked what her responsibility was in terms of her curfew, she responded that she didn't know. She added that she took care of Brian. After much prodding, Alana finally stated that her responsibility was to not stay out late. Kevin felt that a consequence for Alana should be that she would move out. Ann objected, saying that it would be unfair to Brian. The issue was finally resolved by setting different weekday and weekend curfews for Alana. The consequence for violating the curfews was that Ann would not baby-sit Brian. Alana seemed somewhat agitated by this arrangement but still agreed to the consequence.

Throughout the discussion, Alana made very little eye contact and was quite evasive about her responsibilities to Brian. She continually insisted that she didn't understand or that she was confused.

When the family reported for the nest session, they said that Alana had come in at 8:00 one morning, having stayed out all night. Ann told her to move out of the house without Brian. But then she told her that she could stay if she agreed to follow the rules. Ann said that she finally agreed to let Alana stay because she was afraid that Alana would be used by some stranger and because she had been fairly responsible around the house except for the curfew. When questioned by the therapists about what was expected of her by the family, Alana's reply was the usual, "I don't know."

The issue of privacy was then discussed. It had become an issue because Alana always had so many friends at the house. Ann finally worked out an agreement with her that there were to be no friends in the house between 3 and 6 P.M. Ann and Alana also worked out a new curfew schedule and a new consequence for failure to abide by it. Alana agreed to the new rules reluctantly.

At this point the therapists turned the focus of the session to Alan. Alan was hopeful of passing his G.E.D. exam and getting his high school equivalency diploma in June. He was also hoping to receive a $350 scholarship to a local college. He was quite enthusiastic about his new friends at school. When invited to a friend's house for dinner, he had called his mother to report his whereabouts.

At the end of the session the therapists pointed out that Ann was still speaking for the children. For homework they asked Ann and Alana to spend time together, so as to strengthen their alliance and communication. Ann was to continue to work on her expectations for the twins. She was reminded that consequences needed to be reasonable and realistic.

At the following session, it was reported that Alana had once more violated her curfew. As a consequence she was not permitted to go out for four days. When questioned about this, Alana stated that, even though she had not liked staying in, she thought that she deserved the consequence! This was the first sign of any cooperation from Alana. Ann then told Alana that each time she violated curfew, Ann would increase the consequence by one day. To everyone's amazement, Alana agreed with this decision!

Another surprising development was that Ann had talked with Alana's current boyfriend, who had not been aware of the problem of

Alana's staying out too late or of the consequences for violations. Upon learning of the situation, the boyfriend agreed to cooperate and get Alana home by the established curfew.

One further positive happening was that Alana had been getting her friends out of the house between 3:00 and 6:00. This had reduced the tension between Ann and Alana and Alan and Alana. The family seemed to be much more cohesive.

The therapists then suggested that Ann and Alan demonstrate the way in which they talked with one another. Alana was to observe. During this process, Ann retained her tendency to overtalk. However, she was very supportive of Alan's achievements. Alana observed that Alan and Ann were communicating fairly well and seemed to be comfortable with each other. The therapists then asked Ann and Alana to do a model conversation. Ann supported Alana in her progress in G.E.D. classes. She also addressed the issue of the parenting of Brian. She offered to help Alana to toilet-train him, thus making his caretaking a little easier. However, she still continued to lecture at Alana and to cut her off when she was talking. This was pointed out by the therapists.

After the exercise, the therapists asked the family for their reactions. Alana said that it felt good to be able to sit and talk to her mother and that she and Ann did not often do that. She also said that she would like to be able to talk with Ann as a friend. The therapists viewed this statement as an indication of a major attitude change by Alana.

In the last part of the session, the therapists asked Alan and Alana to model a conversation with Ann observing. Although it was difficult to get them to start, Alana was much more assertive in this conversation and also seemed more relaxed and cooperative than at any other time in the sessions. Ann commented that Alan and Alana had been talking with each other more at home and seemed to be enjoying the opportunity to share "teenage talk."

It was noted by the therapists that the family was now abe to joke about the curfew issue. They pointed out that this was an important sign that the issue was now being addressed to everyone's satisfaction, a major improvement in the family's communication process.

Ann arrived alone for session eight. Alana had again broken her curfew. Instead of coming in at 10:30 on a week night, she had come in at 11:45 and then pretended that she didn't know she was late. Ann had told her that whenever she came in after midnight she would keep her in for five days. Alana cried and said that she wasn't coming to therapy any more. Alan also said he would not attend. As Ann prepared to leave for the clinic, Alana had asked her where she was going. Ann replied that she was going to therapy alone. The therapists commended Ann for having taken a strong position. They reminded her to keep referring back to the goals on the assessment card and to be consistent and reasonable.

The remainder of the session was devoted to discussing alternatives for the twins during the upcoming summer vacation. Alan's alternatives were to get a job or to go to live with his grandmother in California. It was suggested to Ann that Alan's getting a job should be the first preference. If that failed, then he might be permitted to stay with his grandmother. Ann was advised against letting Alan sit and do nothing. Then the therapists and Ann discussed alternatives for Alana. Alana's older sister no longer wanted her to baby-sit for her, so the question came up as to whether Alana could find someone to baby-sit Brian while she got a part-time job. The therapists emphasized that the summer could be a critical time for both Alan and Alana. They stressed the importance of Ann's planning her expectations carefully and in advance. It was also pointed out that this should be done in a nonthreatening way. The therapists also highlighted the positive—that Alana was making progress by attending classes and by working to improve her parenting skills. It was further pointed out that it was important for Alana to be able to express her needs.

For homework Ann was asked to set up specific expectations for Alan and Alana for the summer and to come in with a mutually agreed-upon plan by the following week. She was also to decrease her lecturing and monitor her overtalking. If Alana came in before a curfew, Ann was to provide some kind of positive reinforcement. She was to continue to follow through with consequences.

## X. TERMINATION AND FOLLOW-UP

Ann, Alana, and Alan attended the final session. Alana was wearing very little make-up, her hair was arranged in a soft style with no spikes, and she was dressed attractively. The tough look was completely gone.

Ann and Alana had talked over the alternatives for the summer. Alana had agreed with all the suggestions made by Ann, although they had not come to any definite conclusions. Ann had tried to convince Alana to get a job at a fast-food restaurant, and Alana said that she had been thinking about doing the same thing. Alana's social worker had given Alana a new G.E.D. program that she could finish in nine months, so she was looking forward to getting her diploma and possibly going to a computer school.

Alan had told Ann that he wanted to get a job for the summer and that he had a friend who might help him get one at a hardware store.

Alana had surprised everyone by coming in one-half hour before curfew. She said that she was glad her mother had responded positively to that. She said she had told a friend that her mom was getting "really tough." Following up on this remark, one of the therapists pointed out to Ann that her first inclination was to be a softie. Ann agreed but stated that she now felt more in control and believed that she was being fair.

Both Alan and Alana reported that their mother was more calm and that everyone seemed more relaxed. Alan said that he liked the fact that there was more talking and listening. The twins also reported that they had been going out together more often. Ann stated that they had been showing more responsibility and that there had been less "grumping."

In wrapping up the session the therapists asked the family members how they thought they had done so far. Alana said that she thought that all of them had done well. Ann stated that she never would have thought that things could have improved as much as they had.

In closing, the family was told that they now had the tools they needed and that, when they wanted to reduce the tension in the household, they should stick to the basics and go back to the goals on the assessment card. The family members were commended for the great job they had done. Ann began to cry, saying, "I want to thank you from the bottom of my heart." Amid tears and hugs, the session came to an end.

Ann was contacted five months later by the supervisor. During the telephone interview she stressed that the home was more organized with little or no stress between family members. She felt that she was more "planful" about every aspect of her life. The living arrangements remained the same, but Kevin was now used little as a parental consultant. Ann anticipated the return of Alan, Sr., from prison, and she wanted him to blend into the new structure of the family. Alan, Jr., had finished high school with a G.E.D. diploma. He was working part-time and attending first-year classes at a local junior college. Alana still lived at home with her son and cared for her nephew during the day. Ann wanted to continue to help Alana become more independent so that she could move out of her home. Alana had apparently developed more consistent parenting skills and Ann felt much better about how Alana handled Brian. Alana's relationship with her boyfriend was more serious, and they talked about establishing a home together. Alana, however, still had no firm plans for the completion of her education or for employment beyond child care. Ann believed that Alana would have to make the decisions for her own future. The phone interview ended with Ann discussing her wishes for a future life alone with her husband. She felt that they were now ready to become "typical grandparents." She promised to call if she wanted additional consultation.

## XI. THERAPIST REACTION AND EVALUATION

The Smith family members made considerable progress in becoming more structured, more communicative, more open with their feelings, and more confident in their ability to deal with life's problems. They learned to clarify their expectations and needs and to set short- and long-term goals. Each of them left the counseling situation with a greater feeling of self-worth and self-confidence. Ann had become a strong parent. The supervisor rated this family at the top level since its members had accomplished close to 100% of their therapeutic goals.

*Rating*

|  |  |  |  | X |
| --- | --- | --- | --- | --- |
| *1* | *2* | *3* | *4* | *5* |
| no goals attained 0% | few goals attained 25% | half of goals attained 50% | most goals attained 75% | all goals attained 100% |

# CHAPTER 5

# The Isolated
# Family: Stepfamily

## WILLIAM M. WALSH

Therapists: Patricia Bywalec
Janice McIntyre
Supervisor: William M. Walsh

## I. IDENTIFYING DATA

The Salazar family consists of four members. Bing and Carol are in their early forties and have been married for eight years. This is the first marriage for Bing, and the second for Carol. She was divorced ten years ago. Her former husband lives in another part of the country and has periodic contact with her and their two daughters. The two girls had been living with Bing and their mother in a middle-class neighborhood in a single-family home. Rosanne, age eighteen, is now a freshman in a college in another state, in the same locality as her father's present home. He is a well-recognized mental health worker in that community. At the time session one began, she had been away from home for four months. Salina, age sixteen, is a junior at the local high school. Bing and Carol jointly run their own small business from an office in their home.

## II. INTRODUCTORY MATERIAL

The Salazars were referred for counseling by the community hospital after Salina made a suicide gesture by cutting her wrists at home. Initial contact was delayed because of a holiday break, and Salina continued to see the crisis worker at the hospital for four weeks. This relationship was terminated at the beginning of family counseling by mutual consent of all involved in the case. Carol made the initial phone contact. She expressed a desire to identify the cause of her daughter's suicide attempt. The entire family was requested to attend the first three sessions for assessment. Carol stated that since Rosanne was away at school she could not attend the first session but would be present whenever she was in town.

## III. INFORMATION GATHERING (SESSIONS 1 AND 2)

Bing, Carol, and Salina attended the first session. The parents sat together on a couch. Salina chose to sit in a chair close to Bing but at a right angle to the couch. The two therapists sat in chairs that faced the L-shaped arrangement of the family. This was a typical seating arrangement in this room for a first session.

After a brief introduction, the therapists asked the family what brought them into counseling. This was a common opening statement even though the therapists had the introductory information. Bing responded by stating that Salina appeared to be unhappy. He described the incident one month before when Salina had made the suicide gesture. As he spoke, Salina continually interrupted with her perception of the situation. They both agreed that this was her first attempt, and Salina said it was triggered by her feelings of hopelessness. In an attempt to gather as much preliminary information as possible, the therapists asked few questions and provided minimal structure at this time. This gave them the opportunity to observe the family members interact in their "natural" state.

With minimal encouragement, Carol began to interact by describing the problems that she encountered attempting to get Salina to do her chores. The therapists inquired about the rules at home, and Salina described general rules that appeared realistic but inconsistent. Carol then stated that she perceived the "real" problem to be that Salina had a fantasy about her father and wanted their relationship to be closer than it ever could be. When describing her former husband, Carol tensed her body and raised her voice. She became more agitated as she explained her ex-husband's failure to pay child support for ten years. She continued to accuse him of various negative behaviors, and Salina began to defend her father's actions. Bing withdrew physically and emotionally from this conversation until Carol directly asked him to give his opinion. He then attempted to communicate to Salina what Carol had said. Carol and Salina continued their angry exchanges. Both interrupted and blamed the other as the tone of the conversation escalated. Bing once again withdrew and observed the interchanges until both ran out of things to say.

After a brief silence, Carol described her close relationship with her daughter Rosanne and stated how different Rosanne was from Salina. Bing abruptly changed the direction of this conversation by ' tating that Salina had withdrawn from school activities in the past ye r. Carol did not respond, but Salina countered by defending herself and blaming Bing for not being aware of her true activities and involvements. Salina then proceeded to describe her skepticism concerning her mother and stepfather's love for one another, highlighting that she saw her mother as much too dependent on Bing. Their relationship was not her idea of a marriage. She was very outspoken on this issue.

As the session drew to a close, the therapists took a break to discuss a possible homework assignment with their supervisor. Upon reentering, they complimented the family members on the amount of information they were able to report and the courage it took to do so. For homework, Bing and Carol were asked to make parenting decisions together. However, Bing was to actually implement any decisions. Carol was asked to take a break from her role as a parent. In assigning this homework, the therapists were testing the flexibility of the family structure by attempting to restructure the parental roles. The family agreed to try the homework. Carol stated that she needed a break. Bing said that he had never done anything like that before, and Salina liked the idea. The session ended with Carol stating that the family lacked cooperation when doing household tasks. No one responded to this statement since the hour was finished. Rosanne was invited to the next session since she would be home for a school break.

All family members attended the second session the following week. Bing and Carol again sat on the couch, but Rosanne sat between them. Throughout most of the session, Carol and Rosanne sat close together. Carol periodically put her arm around her daughter's shoulders. Salina again chose to sit in the chair close to Bing. The therapists began by inquiring about the homework assignment. Bing reported that the new process had been fairly peaceful and that one argument had been resolved by his intervention. Carol reported that there was less tension in the household. She said that a disagreement between herself and Bing had been diffused when he asserted his role of parent and she withdrew as agreed. Carol described past instances of conflict with Salina over housework. She used blame statements continually when describing each incident. Salina then described her version of each scenario. Blame statements were again in evidence. When Salina was finished, Rosanne gave her version of the incidents. Carol and Rosanne then began to discuss these conflicts, ignoring Bing and Salina. Rosanne defended her mother while highlighting her own helpfulness around the house and indirectly blaming Salina for the problems. Rosanne closed this discussion by stating that definite rules were needed because Salina was lazy and spoiled.

The therapists took this opportunity to focus on the need for rules in the house and the absence of consequences for unacceptable behavior. They stated that they had observed talking and arguing rather than specific, overt consequences for infractions. Bing questioned the practicality of enforcing specific consequences. He stated that Carol often became hysterical and made extreme consequences that didn't "fit the crime." Rosanne defended her mother by saying that Bing was often working and wasn't involved in family disputes. Thus, her mother was overwhelmed and had the right to become hysterical. Carol reinforced her husband's statement that specific consequences couldn't work because "you can't anticipate every infraction."

After a brief silence, Rosanne described her college life and how she gets along well with her roommate because she respects her. She then stated that perhaps definite rules were needed because Carol did get too hysterical and because there was now more arguing going on in the house. Salina then spoke to her parents about how they expected her to act like Rosanne when she was only sixteen and Rosanne was eighteen. She stated that she needed time to grow up and that she would act eighteen when she was eighteen.

The therapists then asked for specific facts about Salina's suicide attempt. Carol described a mood change in Salina the evening of the attempt. She said that Salina had been asking unusual questions and had been more quiet than normal. Carol had asked her to accompany her while shopping, as she was concerned about Salina's mood at dinner. Salina had declined and stayed home by herself. When Carol arrived home late in the evening, she was confronted by several girls in the house. They had been called by Salina to help her attend to several cuts on her wrists. Carol asked the girls to leave and not to discuss the incident at school the next day. Carol then took Salina to the emergency room for treatment. Bing arrived home later that evening after they had returned from the hospital. A hospital crisis worker contacted the family the next day and scheduled an appointment with Salina. Carol further reported that shortly after the incident Salina called her father and threatened to harm herself again.

Salina began to cry in the session. When her mother finished talking, she began to describe her version of the evening. She said that when she tried to hurt herself, she felt that her life would turn out like her mother's and that she didn't want to be like her at all. She stated that she had felt bad but not suicidal when she talked with her father and that she believed he had overreacted to her call.

Rosanne responded to Salina's comments by listing her father's qualifications as a mental health worker who knows when people are at the point of hurting themselves. She believed that Salina had been close to that point. She stated that her father would like the family to work this out together but that he would take Salina to his home if that didn't happen.

The therapists then shifted the focus to a review of the past week. The parents stated that they did try to negotiate expectations but got stuck because Carol was too harsh and Bing was too lenient. Salina had been present during this process but had chosen to add little to the discussion. The therapists suggested that the parents meet privately for further negotiations. They predicted that more arguments would take place as the parents explored each other's ideas at greater length.

Bing stated that he would like Salina to be more involved in future homework assignments. He complained about her inconsistency in moods and completion of chores, as well as her defiance. When asked by the therapists if there were any consequences for this behavior, Bing said that there were not. Rosanne commented that she had accepted her mother's hysterical outbursts long ago and had learned to live with them. She said that she believed that her mother would never change. Carol nodded her head in agreement.

The therapists closed the session by complimenting the family on how well they were doing in and out of the sessions. For homework, they asked Carol and Bing to formulate four or five concrete expectations with appropriate consequences and then to communicate these to Salina as the parental team. Bing restated his desire for homework for Salina. The therapists said that this would occur in the next session.

## IV. INTEGRATIVE EVALUATION

**Structure:**

**Roles:**

**Communication/Perception:**

**Themes:**

**Individual Personality Dynamics:**

## V. FAMILY ASSESSMENT CARD

> The assessment of your family's strengths and weaknesses is based on observation and clinical evaluation by your therapists in consultation with the supervisory staff.
>
> The assessment will provide important information for your family. A commitment by each family member to work on mutually agreed-upon goals both in the sessions and at home between the sessions will maximize the value of this assessment. Work on each of the goals will help your family to function more effectively and help each family member to change and grow.

_____

_____

_____

_____

_____

_____

_____

_____

_____

_____

_____

_____

_____

_____

## VI. COMPLETED INTEGRATIVE EVALUATION

**Structure:**
Comfortable marital relationship with clear boundaries; conflictual parental relationship; Bing isolated from mother in parental decisions; lack of a parental team; coalition between mother and Rosanne; Salina isolated from other family members; conflictual relationship between mother and Salina

**Roles:**
*Expectations:* Unclear and inconsistent
*Consequences:* Unclear and inconsistent
*Follow-through:* Lack of follow-through on expectations for Salina

**Communication/Perception:**
*Communication:* Interrupting by all; blame statements by all; hostile communication between mother and Salina
*Perception:* Poor perception by mother and Salina due to defensiveness

**Themes:**
Hostility between mother and Salina; Carol's resentment toward her ex-husband; Bing's lack of involvement in parental team; fear of rejection by Salina; suicidal gestures by Salina; irresponsibility by Salina due to unclear and inconsistent expectations; Salina's unhappiness and hopelessness

**Individual Personality Dynamics:**
*Carol:* Impulsive, explosive, and defensive
*Bing:* Overrational, withdrawn, uncaring
*Rosanne:* Removed, analytical, "good girl"
*Salina:* Isolated, hopeless, defensive, irresponsible

## VII. COMPLETED FAMILY ASSESSMENT CARD

> The assessment of your family's strengths and weaknesses is based on observation and clinical evaluation by your therapists in consultation with the supervisory staff.
>
> The assessment will provide important information for your family. A commitment by each family member to work on mutually agreed-upon goals both in the sessions and at home between the sessions will maximize the value of this assessment. Work on each of the goals will help your family to function more effectively and help each family member to change and grow.
>
> 1. Carol and Bing need to learn to negotiate their differences regarding parental expectations for Salina and Rosanne.
> 2. Clear expectations and appropriate consequences need to be communicated.
> 3. Each family member needs to practice good listening skills by acknowledging that they understood what the other person was saying.
> 4. Carol and Salina need to express their anger in more appropriate ways; all family members need to decrease blame statements.
> 5. Bing and Carol need to develop ways to be supportive of Salina.
> 6. Salina needs to communicate her needs to her parents.

## VIII. ASSESSMENT SESSION (SESSION 3)

The therapists began the third session by explaining to the family the systems perspective—that problems are interactional, not necessarily individual. Bing, Carol and Salina were present. Rosanne had returned to school. Each family member was given an assessment card which listed the six goals. The therapists went through each goal, explaining it to the family.

Bing reacted first to the information. He stated that he acknowledged his lack of parenting and that he was aware that he needed to be more involved. Carol stated that she, too, would like Bing to become more involved. The therapists initiated a perception check between Carol and Bing. Carol stated that she and Rosanne believed that Bing was stricter with Rosanne than with Salina. The therapists then inquired about the homework assignment. Bing stated that it went well. He then described what he called a "bizarre" incident that had occurred during the week. Salina had gotten cramps while out with her friends. They appeared so severe that an ambulance was called. Bing perceived this as overly dramatic on Salina's part. Salina clarified that she had not wanted an ambulance to be called but was not given a choice. Carol stated that Salina frequently appeared to need medical attention when all she really needed was any kind of attention. She stated that Rosanne had also noticed this. Salina admitted that this could be a cry for attention since she did not feel listened to. She believed that Bing's increased involvement in the family had been very helpful. Bing said that he though it would be depressing for him to always provide the discipline and that he hoped Carol would become less rigid and have more fun with the family. Salina stated that she would like to share her interests with her mother but that her mother never seemed to want to hear about them. At this point, the therapists again stressed the importance of perception checks and practiced this skill with Salina.

The session continued with Carol and Bing discussing some of their expectations for their family. Carol appeared to get defensive and frequently stated that Rosanne agreed with her. Bing appeared calm but passive. Salina then described a situation where she believed that she had been unfairly given a consequence. The therapists related this dialogue with two of the goals on the assessment card regarding communication and dealing with anger.

Toward the end of the session, Carol and Bing were complimented on their work as a parental team. Carol agreed that she might need to "mellow out" slightly. Homework assignments were reemphasized. Bing would continue to give the parental messages to Salina. Carol and Bing were to bring their written expectations to the next session. Perception checks were again discussed, and the family was requested to begin to use them at home. The last part of the homework assignment was for Carol and Salina to spend some positive time together.

## IX. SUBSEQUENT SESSIONS

When the therapists entered the fourth session, they were handed a print-out of the expectations and consequences that the parents had completed on their computer at home. They had listed four types of consequences for negative behavior from Salina and a list of expectations, including how often they wanted them done. The therapists questioned Salina about what she thought of these expectations. She stated that she thought they were "OK" but that the wording was a little too "heavy" for her taste. Carol then said that there had been no opportunity to implement any of them because things were "nice" and there was no reason why this should change. Bing also stated that he had had no opportunity to implement his homework, either. He and Salina had played volleyball together and had had fun.

Carol stated that she had not had any time to have a positive experience with her daughter because it was exam time and Salina had been studying the whole week. Salina stated that she wanted a meaningful relationship with her mother and would like to get past their "chit-chat" conversations. Carol agreed. Salina then went on to say that her mother only enjoyed talking about herself and wasn't interested in anything her daughter had to say. The therapists then asked Salina and Carol to do a perception check with one another. Carol stated that she heard what Salina said and believed that Salina thought this because they still needed to find something to talk about during their time together. The conversation continued, and the therapists encouraged perception checks, as there were many areas of misconception in their communication process. When this issue was resolved, the therapists encouraged them to do perception checks whenever they felt that there might be a misunderstanding. The family members were also questioned about their use of perception checks at home since that had been part of their homework assignment. Bing stated that there had been no opportunity to use them.

The family members then began to compliment one another on the positive week they had had, stating that it had been a long time since they had spent such a nice time with each other. At that point, Carol and Salina began to disagree and to blame each other. The therapists explained what blame statements were and mentioned that the family used such statements continually in their communication process. And so another goal was added to the assessment card, that of reducing blame statements. Family members were asked to become aware of them during the next week. Bing and Carol tried a role-play to ensure that they understood the concept. Other reactions to the assessment cards were solicited. Bing said that he saw communication as the problem that needed the most work.

Salina then asked permission to go on a "tangent." Carol and Bing gave their permission. Salina then expressed her concern about her parents' personal relationship. The therapists explained that, although it was appropriate for Salina to express any concerns she had, the parents needed to have a private life to which Salina should not have access. Salina then asked for reassurance that they loved each other. Carol and Bing both reassured her that they did. Salina then stated that she felt left out of the family because their business was run out of the home, and she had no part in that operation. The session ended with a discussion of possible solutions to this problem. The homework assignments remained the same; Bing and Carol were to work on parenting together, and Bing was to deliver all the disciplinary messages to Salina. Perception checks were to be used with an added awareness of blame statements. Salina and Carol were to continue working on their relationship.

Session five began with Carol and Bing sitting closer together than usual. Carol placed her leg over Bing's and held his arm. When asked about homework, Bing replied once again that there had been very little opportunity to implement it. Carol then stated that there was no need to, as Salina had changed. She has more friends her own age and was less withdrawn. Bing stated that the tension was gone and that that was what they had needed. He continued to say that what they didn't need were formal perception checks. They had tried it once at home, but it wasn't effective because it didn't help them to resolve the conflict.

While describing several incidents of conflict, Carol and Bing stated that Salina "overreacted." When defending herself, Salina would make a blame statement but then catch herself and acknowledge it. Carol would then reluctantly do a perception check. She explained that she was working at not becoming too hysterical. The therapists reinforced all of the changed behavior as it was described. Salina then communicated to her parents that she needed respect and acknowledgment from them, per the goal on the assessment card that she communicate her needs to her parents. The therapists explained to Salina that she could turn a blame statement into a positive communication by saying "I need" before her statement rather than accusing the other person. Salina practiced this skill by telling Carol what she would like from her. When they began to argue, the therapists encouraged them to go back to perception checks. They resisted this intervention. Bing stated that the "fundamental" problem with perception checks was that they didn't help family members to agree. He also stated that Salina was too sensitive and reacted too quickly. The therapists then attempted to explain the differences in perceptions between adults and teenagers. Bing was helped to practice a perception check with Salina. At that point, one of the therapists left the session to consult with the supervisor.

Upon reentry into the session, the therapists explained that both the parental team and Salina had legitimate positions, that one didn't have to be right while the other was wrong. It was further explained that the continuation of blame statements led to a defensiveness that, in turn, led to another blame statement. In this way a pattern developed of one blame statement leading to another. The team suggested that the family make a serious effort to keep track of blame statements and to work on changing them to "I need" statements.

The remainder of the session was spent discussing this feedback. The family was then complimented on how hard each member had been working. The homework assignment was the same with the addition of changing blame statements into positive statements.

The beginning of session six was similar to the previous session in that Carol and Bing were sitting close to each another. Salina sat next to Bing and put her legs on his lap. The family stated that, once again, there had been no opportunity to practice the homework. The members were all very complimentary toward one other.

With the encouragement of the therapists, Salina talked about using a perception check during a volleyball game with Bing. She believed that it had been effective. Carol then stated that she didn't want to have to monitor everything she said by using a perception check.

The therapists then inquired about what changes had occurred to bring about such a positive week. Bing stated that clear communication had helped. Carol stated that Salina was happy, and so the parents were, too. Salina asked that they not put all the responsibility on her. Carol then said that she was also pleased that Bing was helping more with the parenting. The family was confronted by the therapists, who stated that this happy state appeared fragile and that one wrong word could rock the boat. Carol and Bing both disagreed. So one of the therapists left the room to consult with the supervisor. Upon reentry, the therapists said that the team was pleased with the family's progress but that they were concerned about the family alliances when Rosanne returned home. It was stated that the usual alliance was between Rosanne and Carol with Bing distancing himself, thereby isolating Salina. The family was encouraged to be aware of this so that Bing would continue his alliance with Salina. Carol and Bing disagreed about how alliances were formed, but Salina agreed. The therapists reinforced the family system point of view and stated how important it was that Salina not become isolated again. The next session was scheduled for one month later, so that Rosanne could attend, since she was expected home.

Rosanne did not attend the seventh session, as she was back at school. Bing began by stating that the family had changed as much as it could and that now the focus needed to return to Salina. Carol added that Bing and she had talked for hours and had written five pages of notes. Salina stated that her understanding was that they wanted her to lose weight. Bing clarified that they saw this as one way in which she could be more in control of her life. As the therapists asked for clarification, Carol interrupted and stated that she was ready to talk. She then described an incident in which she and Bing had arrived home one evening to find Salina talking on the phone to her father with that "suicidal" look on her face. She said that she felt frustrated because they had done everything that they were supposed to do and Salina was still depressed. Salina responded that she had told her father that her mother and Bing were having marital problems. Carol stated that Salina was being manipulative; Salina defended herself. The therapists called Carol on her blame statement. Carol asked how she should talk to her daughter when Salina is discussing her marriage with her ex-husband. Salina responded that the main conversation with her father centered around her recent use of drugs and alcohol. One therapist then left the session to consult with the team while the other dialogued with the family around this latest issue. When the therapist reentered the session, she drew a structural picture for the family that showed that Salina's alliance with her father invaded Carol and Bing's marital relationship. Carol expressed anger. The therapists pointed out that she had good reason to be angry but that her defensiveness blocked her from communicating effectively. The therapists then inquired as to the status of Salina and Bing's alliance. Bing responded that he felt like he was walking on eggs around her, so he reacted by withdrawing. Salina stated that she would like Bing to approach her occasionally instead of feeling like she always had to approach him first. The therapists talked with Bing about the difficulty he was experiencing with his alliance with Salina. Carol stated that she felt that Salina was jealous of Rosanne because Rosanne had a boyfriend "that she has fabulous sex with." She then added that she had asked Salina to move in with her father. The therapists responded that Salina may have been behaving in a purposefully manipulative manner and that Carol's response had been to blame her. Carol was then asked why she believed that Salina was jealous of Rosanne. She stated that she thought that Salina was "horny." The therapists again observed that blame statements led to defensiveness, which led to other blame statements.

The session continued with Carol and Bing venting their frustrations and the therapists listening to them while attempting to get them back on track with their structural changes instead of regressing to old patterns. Blame statements and Salina's need for an alliance within the family structure were the issues focused on.

After continuous dialogue around these themes, the supervisor entered the session. He stated the importance of the alliance between Bing and Salina and stressed that every time Carol blew up and lost her control, Salina won back control. When her parents felt angry, she won. The more they were able to remain calm, the more her behavior would deescalate. Carol then admitted that she was tired of having to deal with Salina and would like to get rid of her. She also felt angry with her ex-husband and stated that it was time for him to deal with Salina. The therapists suggested that Carol should think of Salina as "winning" whenever she felt anger coming up. A session was then scheduled for the following week, although Salina would not be able to attend as she would be visiting her father for two weeks.

Bing and Carol attended session eight. The focus of the entire session was the parents' need to determine if Salina was mentally ill or not. Her father was planning on doing an informal assessment of her while she was visiting him. If he felt that there were problems with her, he would arrange for a family assessment. According to Carol, the positive aspect of all this was that she had been able to talk and problem solve with her ex-husband for the first time in many years. Bing stated that, if it were determined that Salina was mentally ill, the family members would still proceed with the changes they had made in therapy. Both therapists emphasized that they did not see Salina as mentally ill. A check-up appointment was scheduled for four weeks later. In closing the session the therapists went over the goals on the assessment card to discuss what had been accomplished.

## X. TERMINATION AND FOLLOW-UP

At the ninth and final session Salina, Bing, and Carol all appeared relaxed and happy. Salina had visited her father and was very enthusiastic about the trip. Yet she realized that she wanted to live with Bing and Carol. Carol stated that the therapy had not been helpful in that they did all of the work and the therapists did none. Salina's father had seen no need for a formal evaluation. The family members, including Carol, appeared to be more relaxed than they had ever been since starting therapy. They expressed optimism about their ability to work out family issues in the future. All goals were reviewed and future directions discussed. All agreed to terminate.

Rosanne has since graduated from college and is now living with a friend in the city. Salina is a junior in college and returns home only during vacations. She is working during these breaks and is looking forward to her independence. The parents continue to operate their business from their home. No further need for therapy has been expressed by the family.

## XI. THERAPIST REACTION AND EVALUATION

While the Salazar family members initially presented themselves as a hostile, confused, and frightened group of people, their concern for each other was evident. Once the assessment process was completed, the family members accepted most of the therapeutic interventions. The focus shifted from an irresponsible, self-destructive girl to a malfunctioning family unit. As changes began to occur among family members, new ways of behaving became contagious. The establishment of a new relationship between Bing and Salina was seen as a key point in the therapy. Although Carol remained somewhat impulsive and outspoken, she tempered her statements by a concern for the feelings of the listener. Her statement in the final session about the family doing all the work was characteristic of Carol. It was also seen by the therapists as a comment on their successful but nonintrusive intervention style with all family members.

The therapists and supervisors concurred that the Salazar family had accomplished all of the goals listed on the assessment card and had maintained those goals through the follow-up period. The highest goal-achievement level thus seemed appropriate for this family.

*Rating*

|  |  |  |  | X |
|---|---|---|---|---|
| *1* | *2* | *3* | *4* | *5* |
| no goals attained 0% | few goals attained 25% | half of goals attained 50% | most goals attained 75% | all goals attained 100% |

CHAPTER 6

# The Unblended
# Family: Remarried
# Family

JANICE MCINTYRE
WILLIAM M. WALSH

Co-therapists: Janice McIntyre
Bernadette Veeneman
Supervisors: Paul Farina
William Walsh

## I. IDENTIFYING DATA

The Burke family consists of Paul Burke, fifty-three, his wife Jane, forty-seven, Mike, fifteen, who is Paul's son from his first marriage, and the twins, Judy and Jeannie, twenty, who are Jane's children from her first marriage. Jane has another son, Jim, twenty-three, who lives and works in a different city.

The Burkes are an upper middle-class family who live in a single-dwelling home in the suburbs of a large city. Paul is an insurance broker,

**119**

and Jane is a CPA. Mike attends the local high school, where he is a sophomore. The twins are away at college for most of the year. Jane and Paul have been married for eight years. At the time of their marriage, Jane's daughters lived with them. Mike lived with his mother but spent weekends with his father.

Approximately four years ago, when Mike was eleven, legal custody was changed from his mother to his father, and Mike moved permanently into his father's house. Prior to this change, Mike had lived with his mother from age three, the time of his parent's divorce, to age eleven. Mike's mother is an active alcoholic; Paul is a recovering alcoholic and has been sober since before Mike's birth.

## II. INTRODUCTORY MATERIAL

Paul contacted the clinic to request counseling for himself and Mike. Mike had been having problems at school. He had been cutting classes and getting poor grades. Paul reported that he had had extensive counseling himself for eleven years. In fact, he and Jane were currently engaged in couple counseling. Paul felt that counseling would provide an opportunity for him and Mike to work out their differences and improve the quality of the family life. Jane would not be able to participate, as she had a graduate class that met on the same evening as the counseling sessions. Paul was asked by the supervisors to discontinue the couple counseling while the family was in treatment at the clinic. He agreed to do this and said that Jane would also agree.

## III. INFORMATION GATHERING (SESSIONS 1 AND 2)

The first session began, as it does with all families, with an explanation of the counseling process. Mike was surprised to learn that the sessions were taped and confronted Paul with his belief that Paul had deliberately withheld this information. Mike felt that Paul knew he would not agree to come to counseling if he had been told the sessions were to be taped. Paul denied that he had deliberately misled Mike and said that he had merely forgotten to mention it. Mike stated that the taping was an invasion of his privacy. However, he did agree to sign the release form permitting the sessions to be taped.

Paul stated that he and Jane had recently been involved in couple counseling. They had been working out adult issues, the most compelling one being the ability to offer support and understanding to the other spouse's children. The girls had acted out for a period of time; that issue had subsided, and the current problem was now Mike's behavior.

Mike was asked about his relationship with his stepsisters. It was plain to see that a relationship with them was almost nonexistent. The girls and he merely shared space in the house and spoke only the bare essentials. Mike's main support system consisted of his friends who attended a high school in the city, which was a thirty-minute drive from the family's house. Paul said that Mike had not attended school regularly this year and that his grades were poor. Although Mike thought of himself as a B student, he was currently getting mostly D's. Paul complained that Mike did not do anything at home except "trash-mouth" him and Jane and refuse to help when he was asked to do so. Mike told his Dad that he would like some praise once in a while instead of being jumped on for every small thing that he did not get done. Mike wanted Paul to acknowledge those things that he did accomplish. Paul admitted that Mike was right, that he did not acknowledge those things that his son did right. Paul said that every small thing Mike did threw Jane into a "tizzy" and that he and Jane had been working with the marriage counselor mostly on how to handle Mike.

In the second session Paul discussed Jane's relationship with her daughters. He said they were not together much but that he would term the relationship satisfactory. He believed that Jane had much more energy than did the girls and that they were more passive. Mike added that the girls were "airheads, the kind you marry off to someone." Paul added that he felt that Jane was "on their case" too often. Paul also related that he had been critical of the girls' behavior when they were growing up. He believed that Jane viewed Mike's acting-out behavior as some sort of punishment for Paul's critical attitude toward the girls. Paul said that Jane blamed and judged him for Mike's behavior. He thought that Mike attempted to drive a wedge between himself and Jane by acting out. Paul also described his perception of Jane's feelings about Mike's mother. He said Jane felt that his ex-wife invaded the household through characteristics displayed in Mike's behavior. She believed that the ex-wife "lorded it over" her because of her superior economic and educational background.

Mike then shared his views about male superiority. He believed that the male is "definitely superior" and reported that he became upset when Jane shouted at Paul and when Paul allowed her to have her way. Mike stated that he didn't see his household as a family but that he did respect Jane for her ability to do a lot of things like holding a job, going to school, and keeping house. He also stated that she did a lot of nice things for him such as cooking Sunday dinner and doing his laundry. But at times he was very angry with her and felt that she was "an impossible lady." He also felt angry when she tried to overpower his father. Mike was questioned about his expectations for himself. He said that he wanted to get good grades, be successful, and mainly get his Dad off his back. He realized that he had to do better but said that he had a real problem getting up for classes in the morning. He also said that he never cut classes once he was at school and that the only ones he cut were the first ones in the day. He reported that his grades had steadily declined since eighth grade. Paul said that he expected Mike to attend classes and that he was rewarded with a bonus whenever he attended a full week of school. Conversely, he was penalized $1 per class cut.

Homework for this session was for Mike to decide on his own short-term goals and rewards. Paul and Jane were asked to strengthen the parental subunit by mutually establishing expectations and appropriate consequences for Mike.

## IV. INTEGRATIVE EVALUATION

**Structure:**

**Role Expectations:**

**Communication/Perception:**

**Themes:**

**Individual Personality Dynamics:**

## V. FAMILY ASSESSMENT CARD

The assessment of your family's strengths and weaknesses is based on observation and clinical evaluation by your therapists in consultation with the supervisory staff.

The assessment will provide important information for your family. A commitment by each family member to work on mutually agreed-upon goals both in the sessions and at home between the sessions will maximize the value of this assessment. Work on each of the goals will help your family to function more effectively and help each family member to change and grow.

_____

_____

_____

_____

_____

_____

_____

_____

_____

_____

_____

_____

_____

_____

# VI. COMPLETED INTEGRATIVE EVALUATION

**Structure:**
Rigid boundary between the parental team; rigid boundary around Mike isolates him; conflict in parental unit, lack of parental team; marital conflict due to diffuse boundary between marital and parental subunits; jealousy in marital subunit; mother overly involved with twin daughters—diffuse boundary

**Role Expectations:**
*Expectations:* Not clearly set by parents, lack of mutuality, lack of negotiation by all
*Consequences:* Not clearly stated, lack of mutuality
*Follow-through:* Lack of follow-through by all family members

**Communication/Perception:**
*Communication:* Blame statements made by all; defensive statements by Mike; Paul's communication is inaccurate—his words are stronger than his intended meaning, double messages;
*Perception:* Judgmental statements by all create defensiveness, blocked perception by all

**Themes:**
Paul and Jane do not negotiate differences; family never blended; Mike gets poor grades and cuts classes; Mike's mother is an active alcoholic; lack of a parental team; considerable irresponsibility in all members; continued interpersonal conflict

**Individual Personality Dynamics:**
*Paul:* Recovering alcoholic; passive-aggressive; anger; rigid personality
*Jane:* Rigid personality; refuses to change
*Mike:* Expressed anger, acting out; negative feelings about women

## VII. COMPLETED FAMILY ASSESSMENT CARD

> The assessment of your family's strengths and weaknesses is based on observation and clinical evaluation by your therapists in consultation with the supervisory staff.
>
> The assessment will provide important information for your family. A commitment by each family member to work on mutually agreed-upon goals both in the sessions and at home between the sessions will maximize the value of this assessment. Work on each of the goals will help your family to function more effectively and help each family member to change and grow.
>
> 1. Paul and Jane need to develop and teach each other how to work as a parental team.
> 2. Paul and Mike need to share fun activities together.
> 3. Jane and Paul need to support each other in mutual expectations and consequences for Mike.
> 4. Mike needs to set short-term goals for school.
> 5. Mike needs more positive reinforcement.
> 6. Reduce defensiveness.
> 7. Reduce assumptions by checking perceptions.
> 8. State feelings in clear, descriptive ways.
> 9. Reduce blame statements and negative communication.

## VIII. ASSESSMENT SESSION

Because the third session was a feedback session, it was particularly helpful that Jane was able to attend for the first time. As the family seated themselves, it was interesting to note that Paul sat on the couch and Mike in a chair near the couch. When Jane joined Paul on the couch, she sat nearest to Mike's chair. Mike moved to another chair, commenting that it would be easier to talk across the room. Mike was a very verbal, intelligent young man and had a justification for everything.

Each point on the assessment card was reviewed with the family. Jane and Paul agreed that the first item regarding the parental team was most critical. But they also believed that working as a team could never be accomplished because they could not agree on what was important and what was not. That problem also affected the third item. Jane felt that Paul failed to support her when she thought they had agreed upon expected behavior for the children.

Mike spoke to the second point on the assessment card. He said that he and Paul did enjoy watching sports on TV together but that Jane usually interfered because she wanted the TV off during dinner or because she wanted Paul to do something with her. Jane said that Mike and Paul were usually home alone evenings and did watch TV together but that Mike was resentful any time she made a request for Paul's attention.

The communication items were discussed. Blaming, defending, and lack of clear communication were explained. Paul stated that he felt trapped when Jane asked "why" kinds of questions because he thought that the "why" was judgmental and backed him into a corner. Jane said that she was just trying to understand him when she asked why. Mike could see the purpose for short-term goals, which was the fourth item on the assessment card, but he thought the reference to positive reinforcement, the fifth item, was stupid.

Jane commented that there was a lot of hostility in the household, which came from both Paul and Mike, and that she would like to see that corrected because it was really a terrible way to live. When the discussion turned to the topic of anger, Mike talked about how he really deplored any kind of weak emotion and how he wished that his Dad had taught him how to respond with anger instead of tears while he was growing up. It appeared to the therapists that Mike was scared to death of showing any emotional need and wanted only to express his needs as anger. He was also extremely intolerant of crying and neediness expressed by others. He stated repeatedly that female and feminine traits were worthless.

The family members were asked to name one thing each person would like to see changed in the family. Jane wanted better communication among the whole family. She described the current communication as being "all yelling and hostility." Paul wanted better communication, too. He said that if Jane were angry or hurt, he would like to know why. Mike said he would like to see the morning bathroom schedule worked out so he could have some time without fighting with his stepsisters each morning.

Homework for the following week was assigned. Paul and Jane were to work on mutual parental expectations; Mike was to set short-term goals for himself.

## IX. SUBSEQUENT SESSIONS

Jane was not present at the fourth session. A homework review showed that Paul and Jane had decided upon an expectation for Mike to clean up his messes in the kitchen and basement. If he failed to do so, the consequence would be that he would give up $1 of his allowance per mess left.

Paul and Jane had settled on this item because they could not agree on a more vital or important expectation. Mike set the short-term goal of getting to school on time.

The therapists discussed with Paul the topic of his anger. Paul stated that he was hurt and embarrassed, particularly by Mike's behavior. He admitted to having made comments about the proper way to raise children when Jane's girls were Mike's age. He believed that these comments now had come to boomerang because of Mike's behavior. He told Mike that everything he did "rattled Jane's cage" and that he could not continue to live with them if this behavior did not change. The homework assignment for the next two weeks was for Mike to act pleasantly toward Jane and for Paul to support him.

During the fifth session Paul complained that Mike never said anything positive to any of the other family members. Mike rejected the suggestion of "acting pleasantly" as sounding like "a fairy or fruitcake" and stated that he was not willing to do that. Mike said that his Dad had failed to support him whenever he had tried to be pleasant to Jane. Paul agreed that he had not done that assignment. He was asked to take it for homework for the next week.

The therapists then worked on Paul's communication style. They pointed out to him that he often said things in a much stronger way than he intended. Homework assignments were then restated. An audio tape of the session was sent home to Jane at her request.

Jane joined the sixth session. She had not played the tape from the previous session. Communication issues were discussed. Jane said that she avoided talking to Paul about issues concerning Mike because Paul was so sensitive. Therefore, negotiation within the parental team was difficult. Paul told Jane that he would like to have her address specific behaviors instead of being so critical of him as a person. He said that he heard a message that said, "Paul is a bad guy." The therapists checked to see if Jane had residual resentment from Paul's comments about the behavior of her girls. Jane admitted that she did and seemed unwilling to put the resentments aside.

The therapists reviewed the homework assignment. Jane said that Mike had not been yelling at her since the last session. Paul attributed this to the lack of interaction between Mike and Jane. But Mike said there was a difference, because he had made a great effort to stop yelling at home. Paul said he was still failing to recognize Mike's efforts and to support them. The next homework assignment asked Jane to think of two things that she could do to lower her stress. Mike was to continue to refrain from yelling and to be pleasant to Jane. Paul was to begin to support Mike's efforts.

The seventh session took place four weeks later after the holiday break. Paul and Mike attended. Jane was absent because of an incident with Mike. Paul explained that he and Jane were very upset with Mike because he had chosen to spend Christmas with his mother and did not even call them on Christmas day. Furthermore, he had rejected the presents they had given him except for some cash. Mike reported that he had arranged with both Jane and Paul to have his Christmas gifts in cash this year because he had planned to shop for clothing with his friends after Christmas. He said that clothes were very important to who he was and to how he felt about himself. He stated that they had agreed to this but then had changed their minds without telling Mike. Paul said that Jane was not present at this session because she had totally disengaged from Mike. Paul felt he had done all he could and stated that he was not willing to continue with therapy. The only additional help he was willing to offer was to arrange with a psychiatrist to get Mike on anti-depressant medication. He told Mike, "I cannot live with you any longer. You have as much finesse as a bucket of shit." Mike responded by saying how bad and hurt he felt. He said that he would be willing to talk to Jane to see if she might be willing to return to the therapy sessions if that would help the family to get along better. The therapists supported Mike's feelings. Paul looked doubtful and noncommittal.

The supervisors entered the session when termination seemed imminent. They pointed out that Mike had done the homework and that Paul had not. Jane had not done her homework either. In fact, Jane had not been willing to come to the session because she had disengaged from Mike, but Mike was at the session and had repeatedly done his homework. Yet he was being blamed for the lack of progress. The supervisors told Paul that his decision for an alternative treatment method would be respected but not agreed with. The session ended with the therapists encouraging Paul and Mike to call for another session in the near future.

## X. TERMINATION AND FOLLOW-UP

The premature termination that occurred in the seventh session was unsatisfying for the therapists. They felt that the family members were on the verge of changing their conflictual style and that Mike had been particularly responsive and engaged in the process. Unfortunately, neither Paul nor Jane Burke were willing to continue the process. This, incidentally, had been their style of responding to conflict or challenge in the counseling they had received previously.

One year later, the family and the school counselor were contacted for an update on the case. Paul and Jane were now living alone in the same house and with the same jobs and lifestyle. The twins were away at school and in their own apartment for most of the calendar year. Mike had returned to the city to live with his mother, who was currently in an alcohol rehabilitation program. He had finished his sophomore year with a C average and had then transferred to a school in the city. He was halfway through his junior year with a B average and was reunited with his old friends. Ironically, the initial goals for counseling as stated by Paul and Mike had been met.

## XI. THERAPIST REACTION AND EVALUATION

The largest problem in this case was the lack of commitment by Jane to the process. She was a key element in the family's unhappiness, yet she was not engaged by the therapists from the outset. In retrospect, it might have been more productive to suspend treatment until such time as she was able and willing to be involved.

During the first two sessions, the therapists were led to believe that the only problems Paul and Jane experienced as a couple were those caused by Mike's behavior. This view led to an underestimate of the conflict in the adult subunit. The therapists accurately assessed the presence of conflict and the weak boundaries between the marital and parental units. These permeable boundaries allowed anger from each subunit to affect the other. It was not until the third session, upon meeting Jane, that the therapists realized the extent of the conflict within the marital subunit and Jane's resistance to change. This situation pointed up the need for all family members to be present at the initial sessions. Once this information was received, the therapists were able to focus more on the conflictual marital and parental units. However, Jane's lack of commitment to the counseling process prevented meaningful change from occurring. The main theme, the lack of a parental team, could not be resolved without Jane's full participation. The therapists continued to work with Paul and Mike in an effort to strengthen their relationship, but without Jane's involvement in the process, they were unable to bring about the desired changes.

Mike, on the other hand, demonstrated a commitment to the counseling despite his initial complaints. His openness in the sessions, his willingness to set goals and to do homework assignments, and his desire to continue counseling were seen as indicators of positive growth. In the end, he was the most successful participant and perhaps a more successful person because of that.

*Rating*

X

| *1* | *2* | *3* | *4* | *5* |
|---|---|---|---|---|
| no goals attained 0% | few goals attained 25% | half of goals attained 50% | most goals attained 75% | all goals attained 100% |

7

# The Woman Who Loved Too Much: Single-Parent Family

## THOMAS REAGAN
## WILLIAM M. WALSH

Therapists: Tom Reagan
Bernadette Veeneman
Supervisor: William M. Walsh

## I. IDENTIFYING DATA

Grace Haley is a forty-two-year-old divorcée who is employed full-time as an assistant trust officer at a bank. Her two teenage sons are Steve, age eighteen, an unemployed high school dropout, and Mitchell, age thirteen, an eighth grader at a local elementary school. The third member of the family unit is Olive Johnstone, Grace's seventy-four-year-old widowed mother, who owns the house in which the family lives. Mrs. Johnstone is a full-time homemaker. The boys' father is Dan Haley, age forty-three. He lives nearby and is a partner in a neighborhood tavern. He has occasional contact with the boys.

## II. INTRODUCTORY MATERIAL

Grace's presenting problem was that the boys were acting out at home and not living up to her expectations. She also indicated that the Haleys had been involved previously in counseling, which she reported as unsuccessful.

The family was invited to participate in three information-gathering and assessment sessions. Following the third session, they could decide whether or not to continue.

At the mother's request, one of the co-therapists was male.

## III. INFORMATION GATHERING (SESSIONS 1 AND 2)

Grace and Mitchell were about twenty minutes late for the first session, claiming to be confused about the exact location of the counseling room. No other family members appeared for this session. According to Grace, her mother was ill that night, and Steve refused to come.

The session began with Grace reciting the various reasons why she wanted therapy for her family. Her main complaints concerned the relationship between Steve and Mitchell and between Steve and herself. She viewed Steve and Mitchell as fighting all the time over Steve's tendency to "borrow" money and possessions from Mitchell without Mitchell's permission. She mentioned that Mitchell had become so irritated with Steve over this issue that he had twice threatened him with a knife and was insisting that he needed some way to lock up his possessions. She viewed Steve as believing that, because he was eighteen, he could do as he pleased. He routinely violated her curfew. She reported that all of her efforts to get him to change his behavior (talking to him, taking away his radio and television set, stopping his allowance, locking him out) had proven ineffective. She admitted, however, that she was inconsistent in applying these consequences. She believed that if they didn't work the first time, there was no reason to continue using them.

A second problem for Grace was the interference of her mother in the disciplining of the boys. Reportedly, Mrs. Johnstone was a reclusive person who doted on her grandsons, particularly Steve, and who routinely countermanded Grace's disciplinary efforts. For example, when

Grace withheld Steve's allowance, Mrs. Johnstone would give him money behind her back. Mitchell perceived such conduct by his grandmother as favoritism toward Steve, and he claimed that she never did that for him. Grace also mentioned that her mother always got the boys up in the morning and fixed breakfast for them. If they didn't like what she fixed the first time, she would fix them something else, which resulted in different meals at the same sitting. Mrs. Johnstone also did all the cooking and the laundry, including the laundry of Grace's older unmarried brother, who lived outside the home. Both Grace and Mitchell claimed that, outside of caring for the family, all Mrs. Johnstone lived for was her soap operas on television.

As the recitation continued, the therapists noticed that Mitchell seemed very fidgety and bored with the session. They tried to draw him back into the session by having him confirm what his mother was saying about the family. Mitchell did confirm her statements and added that the family had been in counseling before and that he didn't have much hope that there would be any significant changes. He also restated his perception that his grandmother seemed to always take Steve's side whenever there was trouble involving Steve and other family members. Mitchell resented the way everybody "felt sorry" for Steve whenever he claimed that the family was picking on him.

At this point Grace provided additional information about Steve. He had dropped out of high school in his junior year. Prior to that, he had spent several of his school years in special education classes. He seemed difficult to reach because he kept most of his feelings to himself. He often expressed the belief that his mother and Mitchell were picking on him and was supported in this stance by his grandmother.

Grace also mentioned another area of her life in which she viewed her mother as interfering. Although she had several adult friends, she believed that her mother did not approve of her having a social life outside of the home.

Grace did most of the talking during this first session, and Mitchell gave the appearance of mentally "leaving" the session. The therapists attempted to bring him back by asking him to consider what might be making Steve want to take his things without permission. It was suggested that Mitchell try to find out what was bothering his brother by simply asking him and then listening to what Steve said. The therapists also asked Grace to do two things for the next session: (1) she was to think of consequences that could be applied to Steve for causing fights with Mitchell; and (2) she was to apply those consequences consistently. Both therapists reiterated that the sessions were to start at 6:30 P.M. and that the whole family should try to come. Grace reassured them that the family would be on time because they now knew where the counseling room was.

For the second session, Grace and her mother, Olive Johnstone, appeared and, yes, they were late again, this time by fifteen minutes. Both boys refused to come to this session. Once again, Grace did most of the talking. Mrs. Johnstone proved very difficult to engage in any form of conversation. Grace said that she wanted to be the "perfect parent" and lamented the fact that she appeared to have no control over her family. Of the two boys, she believed that she had a harder time with Steve. However, she also saw Mitchell exhibiting a great deal of "mouthiness" and resistance to doing household chores.

Grace continued her discussion of her difficulties with Steve. She reported that he had held a series of odd jobs since he had left school. During periods of unemployment, he usually moped around the house during the day and partied with his friends at night. Grace stated that she was puzzled about setting consequences and reasonable limits for an eighteen-year old. She reported that, whenever Steve came home after his curfew and found the door locked, he would ring the door bell in order to wake her up to let him in. It was pointed out that such a consequence was really penalizing her and not Steve.

Mrs. Johnstone became involved in the session at this point. She described her role in the family as "chief cook and bottle washer." She stated that she did indeed think that Grace picked on the boys by making them do things that they didn't want to do. She agreed that whenever Grace withheld money from Steve she always gave it to him behind Grace's back.

Grace mentioned that her mother had been suffering recently from a buildup of ear wax, a condition that was affecting her hearing. But Mrs. Johnstone refused to do anything about it.

Grace was asked if her ex-husband had any contact with the family. She stated that he lived close by and was part-owner of a tavern. Mitchell saw his father every Saturday, and he had a job helping to do routine cleanup chores at the tavern. Mr. Haley had very little contact with Steve. When Grace was asked if her brother had a role in this family, she replied that neither she nor the boys were close to him and that they only saw him when he left his laundry for Mrs. Johnstone to do.

At the end of this session, both Grace and Mrs. Johnstone were given assignments. Grace was to formulate a set of expectations and a set of consequences for each of the boys and was to bring this list with her to the next session. In addition, she was asked to give the boys positive reinforcement whenever they lived up to her expectations. Mrs. Johnstone was simply asked to "take a vacation" from child rearing. She was not to interfere with Grace's taking charge of the family structure, and she was to support Grace's disciplinary decisions for both boys. Mrs. Johnstone gave much verbal resistance to this assignment before she agreed grudgingly to give it a try. The next session was set for two weeks, at which time the assessment cards would be handed out and explained, and a decision would be reached about whether the family would remain in counseling.

## IV. INTEGRATIVE EVALUATION

**Structure:**

**Role Expectations:**

**Communication/Perception:**

**Themes:**

**Individual Personality Dynamics:**

## V. FAMILY ASSESSMENT CARD

The assessment of your family's strengths and weaknesses is based on observation and clinical evaluation by your therapists in consultation with the supervisory staff.

The assessment will provide important information for your family. A commitment by each family member to work on mutually agreed-upon goals both in the sessions and at home between the sessions will maximize the value of this assessment. Work on each of the goals will help your family to function more effectively and help each family member to change and grow.

_____

_____

_____

_____

_____

_____

_____

_____

_____

_____

_____

_____

_____

_____

_____

## VI. COMPLETED EVALUATION

**Structure:**
Grandmother invades Mother's parenting role with both boys and undercuts Mother—(diffuse boundaries); parents divorced and father not in the home; little control; conflict between Steve and Mitchell; lack of privacy and respect; Grandmother invades her daughter's adult subunit—(diffuse boundary)

**Responsibility:**
*Expectations:* Lack of clarity or consistency in expectations for the boys; Mom's expectations *are* age-appropriate and realistic
*Consequences:* Lack of consistency in consequences
*Follow-Through:* Steve does not follow through on Mother's expectations

**Communication/Perception:**
*Communication:* Mother and Mitchell have clear communication; Mother communicates with Grandmother but is not heard; Lack of communication between Mother and Steve
*Perception:* Mitchell has clear ideas about how Mother feels; family members don't really listen to each other; much blaming; defensiveness

**Themes:**
Blaming stemming from lack of responsibility by Mother and boys; Grandmother fosters lack of responsibility by doing everything for family members—this creates dependency; Mother and Mitchell feel hopeless and helpless about changing the family dynamics

**Individual Personality Dynamics:**
*Mother:* Frustrated victim of Grandmother, Steve, her job, and, to a lesser extent, Mitchell
*Grandmother:* A recluse who does everything for both her adult child and her grandchildren
*Steve:* The identified patient of the family; a drifter
*Mitchell:* Frustrated victim of Steve and his Grandmother's indifference to him and her favoritism of Steve

## VII. COMPLETED ASSESSMENT CARD

> The assessment of your family's strengths and weaknesses is based on observation and clinical evaluation by your therapists in consultation with the supervisory staff.
> The assessment will provide important information for your family. A commitment by each family member to work on mutually agreed-upon goals both in the sessions and at home between the sessions will maximize the value of this assessment. Work on each of the goals will help your family to function more effectively and help each family member to change and grow.
>
> 1. Mrs. Johnstone can help Mother become more independent and in control by doing less for all family members.
> 2. Open up positive communication by sharing ideas and feelings through talking honestly and directly.
> 3. Work on listening and understanding what each family member is saying.
> 4. Establish clear and consistent expectations.
> 5. Develop and enforce clear and consistent consequences.
> 6. Each person's privacy and possessions need to be respected.

## VIII. ASSESSMENT SESSION (SESSION 3)

For the third session, Grace, her mother, and Mitchell appeared, and they were late again! Each family member was given a copy of the assessment card, which contained recommendations based on information gathered in the first three sessions to improve the family's functioning. The therapists reviewed the six recommendations on the card with the family, stressing that success in solving these problems was the family's responsibility. The therapists then offered to continue working with the family on those points cited on the assessment card. Grace was agreeable, Mrs. Johnstone was noncommittal, and Mitchell was mildly opposed.

The latter half of the session was devoted to listening to Grace's problems with Steve, Mitchell's reaction to his grandmother's favoritism of Steve, and Mrs. Johnstone's general unhappiness with having to sit back and let Grace discipline the boys by herself. Grace then mentioned that she had discovered drug paraphernalia in Steve's room and was concerned about what to do. Her initial response to this discovery was a reluctance to set consequences for Steve, even though she realized that she must do so for the good of the family. Mrs. Johnstone's affect was one of silent defiance, apparently in reaction to the suggestion from the previous session that she take a vacation from disciplining the boys. Mitchell felt that the best solution was to kick Steve out of the house. He became angry and stated that he wanted to discontinue counseling when it appeared that his suggestion was not going to be followed. Grace's assignment for the next session was to think of consequences for Steve's having drug equipment in the house and to apply the consequences consistently. Mrs. Johnstone was to think of something nice to do for each member of the family. The family would be seen in a week.

## IX. SUBSEQUENT SESSIONS

The fourth and fifth sessions, which took place at weekly intervals, showed just how ambivalent Grace was about setting expectations for the boys and consequences for their failure to abide by them. They also revealed Mrs. Johnstone's reluctance to stop "spoiling" the boys and her fear that she would have no place in the family structure if she changed her way of treating them. Mitchell did not attend the fourth session but did come to the fifth session, which proved to be his last appearance. He and Grace had continued to argue over Steve's doing as he pleased at home and Grace's inability to enforce consequences for Steve's misbehaviors. Mitchell also admitted that he was getting tired of authority figures in general because of his mother's "wishy-washiness" with Steve. But Grace finally produced written lists of expectations and consequences for both Steve and Mitchell during the fifth session. They seemed to be a source of controversy between Grace and Mitchell, as well as between Grace and her mother. There was also the ongoing controversy over the issue of separate rooms for the boys. A room was being built for Steve in the basement, but there seemed to be delay after delay in getting it finished. This, too, was adding to the general conflict at home. In both sessions the therapists supported Grace in redefining her role as Mother in the family. Although they tried to explain that role to Mrs. Johnstone, she continued to passively resist any effort to restructure her place in the family.

The sixth session produced a surprise. Steve came with his mother and grandmother. Grace had established attendance at counseling as a contingency for Steve's having his own room. Steve explained his presence by stating that he wanted that room. He presented a very shy and withdrawn young man who was unhappy with his home situation and wanted to be on his own. However, money was a problem for him because of his sporadic employment and his lack of a high school diploma. Grace admitted that the home situation was generally chaotic, with Steve and Mitchell fighting frequently and with Mitchell's mouthiness increasing and his general attitude deteriorating. Grace stated, "I'm an overprotective mother . . .who doesn't do discipline well . . . who needs to please." She also admitted that she set up consequences that she could not enforce. It was suggested that she had an underlying fear of displeasing her boys if she did so. However, she was able to confront Steve about his drug paraphernalia, but he claimed that he didn't know it was there. He also tried to convince his mother that he needed her help in dealing with Mitchell, whom he viewed as very disrespectful of him and against whom he had built up an anger of several years' duration. Once again, Mrs. Johnstone just seemed to take up space and didn't respond to the conversation except to say, "I just don't know." The therapists were able to get Grace to verbalize her current expectations of Steve. These included no illegal substances in his room, keeping his room in the basement clean, and asking Mitchell for permission to borrow his things. Grace's homework was to finish going over other expectations and consequences with Steve at home.

The seventh and eighth sessions found Grace getting somewhat stronger about setting consequences for the boys' behavior. However, she mentioned that, although Steve actually seemed to be responding to this, Mitchell was beginning to act out. Both therapists pointed out that these changes in the boys' behavior indicated that the family routine was changing and that Grace should continue to enforce her consequences consistently and unemotionally. They predicted that troubles would continue for awhile until the boys could see that Grace meant what she said, at which time she would begin to notice gradual improvement. She stated that the fact that the boys now had their own rooms was somewhat helpful. Mrs. Johnstone mentioned that she also thought Mitchell was upset about the changes, but she didn't think he was as "mouthy" as he had been before. She saw Steve as "unreachable" because he was now in the basement. She continued to express general unhappiness with all the changes. Once again, the therapists stressed the need for expectations and consequences to be applied consistently and unemotionally.

For the remainder of the sessions, Grace was the only participant, as both Mrs. Johnstone and the two boys refused to come. This development presented the therapists with an opportunity to help Grace examine her own feelings and attitudes and to make those changes in her life that would help her to become a stronger person in her own right. It was expected that such changes would prove helpful in her efforts to continue to set expectations and consequences for her sons.

During these individual sessions, Grace provided information about her past and about her current functioning. She reported that she had married her husband when she was nineteen and that he was an alcoholic for whom she continually made excuses until the marriage fell apart. In general, Grace felt taken for granted and believed that her opinions and feelings didn't count. She also believed that her work supervisor took advantage of her and her willingness to see a project through until it was completed. Although she was interested in dating, she felt guilty about having fun when she perceived herself as having so much work to do around the house. She also stated that she realized that she was overly protective of her sons and that she couldn't bear to sit back and watch them take the consequences of their actions. However, Grace discussed an incident that demonstrated her increasing ability to set limits on Steve's behavior. She had discovered a drinking party going on in Steve's basement room. She asked his friends to leave and told Steve that he couldn't have friends over again until she said he could. Grace reported that Steve responded favorably to this limit setting.

In the ninth session, the therapists and Grace discussed the desirability of her distancing herself emotionally from her mother and her sons so that she could be more objective in dealing with them. A secondary reason for this suggestion was to establish more appropriate boundaries between the subunits. Grace was reminded that she needed to keep giving her expectations and consequences objectively and unemotionally for maximum effectiveness and that she was to make them clear and concise from the start. She mentioned that she was dating again but was afraid of a permanent relationship with a man because of her disastrous marriage. A four-week holiday period ensued.

There were six more sessions with Grace during a four-month period. During the tenth session Grace told the therapists that she was "a woman in love" and that her gentleman friend and she had spent quite a bit of time together over the Christmas/New Year's holidays. She admitted to being afraid to commit to a permanent relationship with him because she had been burned before and because he was "more of a perfectionist" than she was. Yet, she was pleased that Mitchell had responded positively to him. It also came out that she and Mitchell had argued over some minor matter at home and that he had left home without permission between 12:30 and 3 A.M., for which he had lost his allowance. Grace was reinforced by the therapists for knowing what to do in terms of expectations and consequences in this incident. Grace also mentioned that she believed that her mother was not happy about her relationship with Sam.

It was agreed that at the next session attention would be given to Grace's attempts to control her own life and to meet her own needs. It was hoped that, by having Grace focus her attention on her own life, the adult subunit of Sam and Grace would continue to develop.

Within a four-week period, there were three more sessions. During this time Grace continued to expound on how difficult it was for her to put her own needs and wishes ahead of those of others. At the same time, workload problems were beginning to crop up at her job, and she felt she was being squeezed by a supervisor who was leaving and by a subordinate who was being rushed to learn all the essentials of the job. Grace also revealed that her relationship with Sam was deepening and that this pleased both her and Mitchell but not Steve or her mother.

During the twelfth session, the therapists focused on the concept of the family structure, including subunits and boundaries. They made a chart showing the adult, parent, and sibling subunits of the family system. It was pointed out to Grace that no one unit should interfere with the functioning of any of the others. In other words, Grace's relationship with Sam should not be the business of the boys or of her mother. Additionally, Grace's function as a parent to the boys should not be interfered with by her mother or anyone else unless Grace herself called for assistance.

There were additional positive developments. When Mitchell and an older friend went to a late movie on a school night without Grace's permission, she contacted Sam, who suggested that she go to the theater and bring Mitchell home. This incident demonstrated Sam's entrance into the parental subunit. And Grace did indeed have Mitchell home before he had intended to be there! When Steve developed a skin rash that concerned Grace, she was able to follow the advice of the therapists that she allow Steve to live with it until he himself felt the need to do something about it.

During the thirteenth session the supervisors entered. Grace had been giving her familiar tale of woe about her inability to set consequences for her boys' misbehaviors, her tendency to take on too much responsibility, and her need to please other people. The supervisors pointed out that Grace's need to please others resulted in her taking on too much responsibility for their reactions, good or bad, to her limit setting, and that this was impeding her efforts to set appropriate consequences. Her overresponsibility also affected her relationships with her mother and with her boss. All of these things were causing her to feel helpless and hopeless, primarily because she was putting the wishes and demands of her boss, her mother, and her job ahead of her own. They also pointed out that Grace already knew what she needed to do to regain control over her life, and that these attitudes were impeding her progress.

Focusing on these Individual Personality Dynamics created a point of major, positive change in Grace's therapy.

The next session was set for four weeks later. Grace's homework was to continue to create meaningful consequences for the boys' misbehavior. It was suggested that, as her relationship with Sam continued to deepen, she should feel free to use him as a consultant if she wished, so long as she retained the final say over disciplinary matters.

What a difference four weeks can make! During the fourteenth session, Grace informed the therapists that she had taken a week's vacation to Florida with Sam. The trip was on short notice so, before she left, she had presented a list of expectations to her family. To her delight, her mother did not interfere with the trip and, while Grace was gone, followed Grace's instructions concerning the boys. Both Steve and Mitchell were exhibiting better behavior at home and both were becoming more accepting of Sam and of their mother's relationship with him. The therapists reinforced Grace for the way she had taken charge of the situation. They also mentioned the intrapsychic obstacles to success that the supervisors had pointed out in the previous session. Grace replied that she realized what they were and that they were not affecting her at the present time. Her relationship with Sam on an adult level was developing nicely. Since the following session was to be the termination session, Grace was asked to include Sam so that he could be updated about the issues with which Grace had been dealing. Homework was for Grace and Sam to discuss their future plans, since marriage was now a distinct possibility. In that context, they were to begin to plan for Grace's mother and the boys about where they would all live, and for themselves as an adult subunit.

## X. TERMINATION AND FOLLOW-UP

Grace and her good friend Sam appeared for the fifteenth session. The therapists showed Sam the diagram of the adult, parent, and sibling subunits in the family structure to help him see what Grace had been working on since last September. He understood and supported her work. Although Grace and Sam were close to a decision concerning their engagement and marriage, they had not yet done a lot of concrete planning for her mother or the boys. Sam pointed out that he had two adult daughters and an aging mother, who was living with his sister. Therefore, he felt that he was able to understand Grace's problems concerning her family. Grace had given living arrangements some thought and was leaning towards leaving her mother's home if she and Sam were to marry. She felt that Mitchell, because of his age and positive feelings towards Sam, would probably live with them. Steve would be welcome to live with them, to live on his own, or to live with his grandmother. Grace mentioned that both boys were now more responsive to her wishes and were more respectful of her directions. There were still occasional lapses, but, in general, the atmosphere at home seemed much calmer. Steve was exhibiting a great deal more willingness to help out around the house and was expecting to return soon to his landscaping job. Mitchell seemed to be taking more responsibility for his school work. He planned to graduate that June from elementary school. Sam indicated that he noticed that things in Grace's home seemed calmer and quieter. Grace claimed to be spending more time providing for her own needs, as the trip to Florida illustrated. Grace also said that her mother appeared to be much more respectful, not only of her relationship with Sam but, more significantly, of her parental role with the boys. She had shown lately that she was not so eager to "spoil" the boys as she had once been. Furthermore, she continued to follow Grace's wishes for the boys when Grace was away from home.

The therapists reviewed the assessment card with Grace and Sam, noting the positive changes that had occurred since last October. As the session terminated, Grace was reminded that she had the ability to keep herself on track with the goals on the assessment card and that she was capable of setting up expectations and consequences. Finally, as they departed, Grace was told that she could return if she felt she was slipping or needed reinforcement.

## XI. THERAPIST REACTION AND EVALUATION

Grace Haley may have felt she was a helpless and hopeless victim of her family and her job in September when counseling began. But her tremendous motivation to change and her persistence in continuing with the counseling sessions alone helped her change both her own self-image and the way she dealt with her family. Therefore, Grace was gradually able to change from helpless victim to competent adult and parent. She was able to set expectations and consequences and to have them respected and followed without interference from her mother or her sons. Although it would have been helpful for both the boys and Mrs. Johnstone to participate more often, it really was Grace's motivation and positive response to the sessions that brought this case to a successful conclusion. The therapists were instrumental in facilitating change, but it was the "woman who loved too much" who actually did it!

*Rating*

|  |  |  | X |  |
|---|---|---|---|---|
| *1* | *2* | *3* | *4* | *5* |
| no goals attained 0% | few goals attained 25% | half of goals attained 50% | most goals attained 75% | all goals attained 100% |

# CHAPTER 8

# The Parent Who Couldn't: Single-Parent Family

JANICE McINTYRE
WILLIAM M. WALSH

Therapists: Janice McIntyre
Tom Reagan
Supervisors: Marge Jennings
William M. Walsh

## I. IDENTIFYING DATA

The members of the Potter family are Louis, age fifty-one, and his son Allan, age fourteen. Louis and Allan live together in an apartment on the outskirts of a large city and have done so for about four years. Lou has been separated from Allan's mother for six years. Allan has two sisters—Clara, age sixteen, and Nora, age thirteen—who live with their mother. This part of the family lives close enough so that the children visit each parent at least once a week. This living arrangement appears to be satisfactory to all family members. This marriage had been Lou's second. He has two married daughters and one granddaughter from his first marriage.

Lou is a hairdresser and is very happy at his profession. Allan is a sophomore at a local high school.

For a period of three years Lou had a girlfriend who shared the apartment with Lou and Allan. Allan agrees that the three got along very well. Lou felt a little sad when she left but also felt that because of the issues between them the parting was OK. He believes that he grew from the experience. Allan stated that he missed her but that her moving was "no big deal."

## II. INTRODUCTORY MATERIAL

Lou had requested counseling several months earlier, but the clinic was at capacity and unable to accommodate him at that time. Several weeks later, when he learned that it was accepting new clients, he contacted the clinic office regarding parenting and relating problems that he was having with his son. In addition, he reported that his son was cutting classes and that there had been a recent incident with a gym teacher.

## III. INFORMATION GATHERING (SESSIONS 1 AND 2)

Lou stated that he wanted to achieve a better working arrangement and understanding between himself and Allan. He said that Allan was having a difficult time with school rules, grades, and attendance. Lou admitted to feeling a lot of anger toward Allan. He felt that Allan demonstrated a lot of anger toward him.

Allan's mother and sisters lived a short bus ride away. Lou reported that, in the four years that Allan had been living with him, the boy would go to his mother with any issue that came up between father and son. Lou's estranged wife would then call Lou and scold him as though he were her child. This, Lou felt, was unfair because he did not interfere in the raising of his daughters. He believed that his ex-wife's household was in worse turmoil than was his own and thought that the other part of the family should be in counseling as well.

The therapists encouraged him to ask the others to join in the sessions. But after rethinking the matter, Lou decided he didn't want them present until he had a better handle on his relationship with Allan. He feared that the whole group together might create chaos. The therapists were unable to persuade him otherwise.

Lou's chief complaint was that he had no control over Allan. He thought that he communicated his expectations clearly, but Allan paid no attention to his father and behaved any way that suited him, regardless of his father's wishes. The result of Allan's failure to do as he was told was a long history of wailing and berating by Lou.

Lou reported that Allan had stolen things since he was a child. Once he had stolen $100 from one of Lou's employees, and Lou had to pay it back. Lou felt that Allan didn't feel sorry for the embarrassment and financial problems he had created for his father, and Lou was still angry about the situation. He said that Allan did not relate to him in any way and that he knew that anything he said to his son was just words to which Allan paid no attention. Lou was at a loss as to what to do next.

Allan then discussed his life. He reported that he didn't go to school much because he didn't really like it. Grades on his last report card were two D's and the rest F's. When he went to school he did his homework in class or in study hall. After school he joined his friends to just hang out. Allan was not expected home for dinner. He came home from school but was gone before his father got home by 4:00 or 5:00. He returned home by 9:30 on weekdays and 10:30 on weekends.

Homework for this sessionn was for Lou and Allan to find a time each day when they could get together and just talk and share the happenings of the day. They agreed, Allan reluctantly.

In the second session Lou related an incident in which Allan was given a one-day suspension from school. Allan had chosen to use the toilet facilities at a nearby restaurant rather than those at school, claiming that the school restrooms were not clean. He was suspended for leaving the school without permission. In relating the story Lou stated that he thought that Allan should have used the facilities provided by the school, that they were indeed adequate, but that the school was also wrong for issuing the suspension. He felt that the penalty was too severe for the infraction.

Lou also talked about his own family background. His mother, although not well, was still a very controlling woman. Lou was feeling a great deal of resentment toward her. Reportedly, she continued to be an unbending, blaming, and unreasonable woman. Lou said that he wished that she were dead. He stated that his love for his work had pulled him through many difficult problems throughout his adult life.

## IV. INTEGRATIVE EVALUATION

**Structure:**

**Roles:**

**Communication/Perception:**

**Themes:**

**Individual Personality Dynamics:**

## V. FAMILY ASSESSMENT CARD

The assessment of your family's strengths and weaknesses is based on observation and clinical evaluation by your therapists in consultation with the supervisory staff.

The assessment will provide important information for your family. A commitment by each family member to work on mutually agreed-upon goals both in the sessions and at home between the sessions will maximize the value of this assessment. Work on each of the goals will help your family to function more effectively and help each family member to change and grow.

_____

_____

_____

_____

_____

_____

_____

_____

_____

_____

_____

_____

_____

_____

## VI. COMPLETED INTEGRATIVE EVALUATION

**Structure:**
Rigid boundary between father and son; lack of communication and perception between father and son; diffuse boundary between Allan and Mother; diffuse boundary between Lou and ex-wife, who interferes in his parenting; lack of a parental team; Allan uses Mother against Father; chaotic parenting in Mother's home; inadequate parental behavior by Father; inadequate role models for Allan in both families

**Roles:**
*Expectations:* Inadequate expectations for a fifteen-year-old; inconsistent expectations; expectations not clearly stated by father
*Consequences:* Allan ignores expectations and consequences; few consistent and realistic consequences
*Follow-Through:* Little or no follow-through

**Communication/Perception:**
*Communication:* Lack of positive communication; much yelling; father gives double messages about son's behavior
*Perception:* Poor perception—both claim that the other doesn't listen

**Themes:**
No mutual nourishment between father and son; father and son have much anger toward one another; Allan is raising himself—comes and goes as he pleases; Allan seeks emotional support outside the home; Lou lacks control of Allan; Lou treated as inadequate and childlike by his ex-wife; Allan exhibits acting-out behavior in and out of school

**Individual Personality Dynamics:**
*Lou:* Fear and resentment over controlling mother and ex-wife; overinvolved in work; feels helpless and inadequate; uses passive–aggressive behaviors, like resisting suggestions
*Allan:* Resistant to authority; acting-out behavior; emotionally isolated from father; manipulative

## VII. COMPLETED FAMILY ASSESSMENT CARD

The assessment of your family's strengths and weaknesses is based on observation and clinical evaluation by your therapists in consultation with the supervisory staff.

The assessment will provide important information for your family. A commitment by each family member to work on mutually agreed-upon goals both in the sessions and at home between the sessions will maximize the value of this assessment. Work on each of the goals will help your family to function more effectively and help each family member to change and grow.

1. Clear boundaries must be established between parental and child subunits.
2. Father needs to establish clear and consistent expectations.
3. Father needs to develop and enforce clear and consistent consequences.
4. Allan needs to learn about roles in family structure.
5. Allan needs to understand his home and school responsibilities.
6. Both Allan and Lou need to focus on positive communication by sharing ideas and feelings directly.
7. Both need to increase listening and understanding of what the other is saying.

## VIII. ASSESSMENT SESSION (SESSION 3)

The third session began with a homework review. Lou and Allan told the therapists that circumstances prevented them from doing much about the homework assignment of making time for some talking and sharing. Lou had gone camping during the week; Allan had been sick in bed for a good part of the time when they were at home together.

The therapists told the family that when expectations are clearly established, consequences must also be clear and understood by all. Lou replied, "My mind doesn't work that way." The therapists then discussed the importance of commitment as demonstrated by doing the assigned homework. The items on the assessment card were reviewed with the family. Both members agreed there was a need for better communication. Allan said that his dad did not listen to him. There was minimal reaction to the other items. Homework was then assigned for the following week. Each was to bring in written expectations that they had for the other family member.

## IX. SUBSEQUENT SESSIONS

At the following session Lou brought in his list of written expectations, but Allan did not. The therapists asked Allan to do this assignment for the next session and supported his efforts.

Lou then stated that he hoped that Allan would grow up to be happy and successful and that he saw his role as parent limited to giving advice. He felt that if Allan respected him as a parent he would do what Lou asked of him. Allan said that his hopes for himself were to be a chef or play in a band or to be a commodities broker. He realized that he wasn't on the road to achieving any of these things. He said that, since he wasn't currently getting passing grades, he planned to make the most of his classes the next year. He also said that he was not considering summer school because it was inconvenient. The therapists then pointed out that Allan needed his father's support and that one way Lou could provide that support was to set consequences as a means for Allan to grow and learn to accept responsibility. The homework assignment was for Lou to think of two or three consequences that he could use when expectations were not met. The therapists explained that it was absolutely essential for Lou to take this step at this time.

Lou showed up at the next session alone. He said that Allan had been picked up by the police for breaking into a parking meter canister. Allan's story had been that the canister was lying on the sidewalk and that he and his friends were caught opening it. Lou said that the trouble was that he couldn't believe his son. He related an incident from the previous year in which Allan and some of his friends found a key to their downstairs neighbor's apartment, stole household items from the apartment, and brought them to another friend to be fenced. The items had been recovered the same day and no charges had been made because of the age of the children and because the victims were friends. Another incident occurred when Allan was twelve. He was picked up for breaking into the coin box of a newspaper dispenser. Again, no charges had been filed because of Allan's age. When he was eleven, he stole $100 from the cash box of Lou's employer. Lou said that he yelled and screamed after each incident. He was very hurt and angry. But no consequences were ever applied.

The therapists told Lou that what he had been describing was a pattern of lawbreaking that would have to be interrupted at once. Something different in the way Lou was handling his parenting job would have to happen. Lou said that, if his son loved and respected him enough, he could control him. The therapists replied that Lou could earn respect when he showed Allan that he loved him enough to establish control. They asked Lou if he really wanted to control Allan. If he did, he needed to learn the techniques that were suggested to him. They also wondered whether it was possible that Lou did not really want to take control. It was explained to Lou that if he really did not want to take control he couldn't be forced to do so. Lou assured the therapists that he really did want control. He stated that maybe in some way he was hoping that the school and the counselors there would make the changes for him but that he now realized that he had to do it himself.

During the sixth session Lou said that he was experiencing a great deal of stress. He had financial burdens that he could not meet, in addition to his problems with Allan. Fees for Allan's attorney were due. He had also learned that he would have to provide funds for his sick mother.

The issue of controlling Allan was again raised. The therapists appealed to Lou's love for Allan in encouraging Lou to establish both positive and negative consequences for his son. Lou became very negative toward Allan. He said he believed that Allan had a "criminal primal essence" and that, if he continued in his present pattern, he would live his life in prison. He felt that if that was what Allan chose to do, he should be allowed to continue with his life as he saw fit. At this point the supervisor entered the session. He emphasized to Lou that, unless he was ready to accept his role as parent and develop consequences for inappropriate behavior, therapy was not likely to be of any help to him. Lou replied, "I would rather be a tough parent with control than a screaming parent without control, but somewhere in the back of my mind there's a voice saying that this whole thing is a crock of shit."

The homework assignment for Lou was repeated. He was to think of consequences and write them down. Lou's reaction to this assignment was that he felt that he was right back at the beginning and that his mind still did not work in terms of consequences.

## X. TERMINATION AND FOLLOW-UP

Lou came alone for the seventh and final session. He said that before the arraignment for the first offense had occurred Allan had been arrested again. This time the offense was for attempted auto theft. He stated that he did not want to sit and listen to the therapists telling him that he wasn't doing something, that he wanted Allan to have individual therapy. The therapists explained that parental control must be established through the use of consequences. Lou agreed that establishing consequences would be fine when Allan came back and if he was willing to work with his father and the therapists. The therapists agreed that therapy could be discontinued at that time and reestablished later, but they insisted that all homework assignments had to be completed by both Lou and Allan. Lou said that he would agree to do so if Allan agreed to therapy.

The supervisor again entered the session. He explained that Lou's lack of control was a long-standing problem and that Lou could not expect immediate results. He said that results would be seen only when consequences were clear, consistent, and repeatedly applied over time. He told Lou that Allan's belief that his behavior would not result in consequences had been reinforced through the counseling process, because Allan could see that his father had been unwilling to establish consequences, even when to do so had been a homework assignment.

Lou was then reassured that the door would be open for him and Allan should they wish to reengage at a later time.

## XI. THERAPIST REACTION AND EVALUATION

In retrospect the therapists noticed two themes that, had they been dealt with, might have contributed to a more favorable outcome. First, the therapists should have insisted more strongly that all family members attend the therapy sessions. Allan's mother and sisters played a pivotal role in influencing the father-son relationship. Without their presence, it was difficult for the therapists to change the dynamics between Lou and Allan. Secondly, Lou's IPD showed that there was a probable connection between his deep anger toward his extremely controlling mother and his inability to set consequences. It was likely that Lou viewed consequences as controlling and believed that if he set consequences he would become the controlling parent that he hated.

Lou's personal inability to take responsibility for his son and, in a larger sense, for his own life, fostered the continued irresponsibility of Allan. Lou had always depended on others—mother, wife, girlfriend—to make decisions and carry out actions. At the same time he resented their dominance and control. Lou abdicated his role as parent and expected others in authority to control Allan for him. Without changes in Lou's personal feelings and attitudes, interpersonal interventions were ineffective. Lou was the parent who couldn't because he was the person who wouldn't—wouldn't change his personal belief and behavior system.

But despite the difficulty that Lou experienced with his son and female figures in his life, he was able to gain greater insight into his own
behavior and that of those around him. At termination he spoke of his
desire to change in the future, because he now realized how his behavior
affected other people. Even though he was unwilling to continue the present counseling, the supervisor felt that minimal changes had occurred and
therefore rated this case at the 25% level.

### Rating
          X

| 1 | 2 | 3 | 4 | 5 |
|---|---|---|---|---|
| no goals attained 0% | few goals attained 25% | half of goals attained 50% | most goals attained 75% | all goals attained 100% |

# PART IV

# Families with Adult Children

# 9

# Time After Time: Single-Parent Family/Lover

## WILLIAM M. WALSH
## BERNADETTE VEENEMAN

Therapists: Thomas Reagan
Bernadette Veeneman
Supervisors: Pamela Ligman
William M. Walsh

## I. IDENTIFYING DATA

The Sommers family consists of Sue, the mother, age forty, Robert, her live-in boyfriend, age thirty-three, Marcy, age twenty, Dick, age eighteen, and Cathy, age sixteen. An older daughter, Shelly, age twenty-two, lives in South Carolina with her husband and has little contact with the family.

Sue has been divorced for ten years and works as a receptionist in a small suburban firm. Robert, also divorced, has a four-year-old daughter and is a construction worker. Robert is known to be a heavy drinker by both family and friends. Dick and Marcy are both high school dropouts. Marcy works with a maintenance crew for a local bank, and Dick

**161**

works part-time as a salesperson. Cathy is a junior in high school and a part-time stock person at a card shop.

The family lives in a three-bedroom apartment in an undesirable neighborhood of a large city. The apartment is too small for the family plus the guests that Dick and Marcy constantly bring home.

## II. INTRODUCTORY MATERIAL

The Sommers family was referred for therapy by Cathy's school counselor. Cathy appeared very unhappy at school and had repeated tardies and poor grades. When approached by the counselor, Sue and Robert both agreed that the family needed counseling. Sue wanted to come to therapy because of the friction in the home; Robert wanted to come because the children were not respectful toward him.

## III. INFORMATION GATHERING (SESSIONS 1 AND 2)

The Sommers family was on time for the first appointment. Although the members were all encouraged to attend each week, this was the only session for the entire family. They were all visibly nervous as they took their seats in the therapy room. They were uncomfortable with the idea of being videotaped but did sign a consent form. Cathy wanted to know if she could view the tape and was relieved to know that she and anyone else in the family could view the tape if they gave sufficient notice. With the forms signed and introductory material gone over, the family seemed more comfortable and willing to work.

Robert started by talking briefly about himself. He reported that he was a construction worker employed in the suburbs and that he liked his job. He stated that he was originally from Pennsylvania, where his four-year-old daughter Tracy now lived with his former wife. His mother also lived in Pennsylvania. He saw his family about two or three times a year. With the help of his brother, he had moved to his present city from Las Vegas, Nevada, the previous year. While in Nevada he had been picked up for drunk driving. He had met Sue in a restaurant after moving to his current city and reported that they "hit it off real good." They dated from July until September, and then he moved in with Sue and her family. Sue and Robert were engaged at Christmas time of that same year. He wanted to get married in the near future, but they both agreed to postpone the wedding because of problems between Dick and Robert and also because of family financial problems.

Cathy, who was sitting next to Robert, spoke next. She stated that she was a junior at a local high school. Then she said, "There's too much to say." She looked tense and kept tapping the microphone with her foot. She continued by saying that she had recently lived in New York for one year with her friend Margaret and Margaret's mother. She got along well with Margaret's mother and talked with her each day after school. However, Margaret did not like their relationship. Cathy said that Margaret was jealous and made life miserable for her. Cathy said, "She ruined me emotionally." But she gave no details about what she meant by that. She stated that she had originally moved to New York because she and Margaret had been best friends when they lived in North Carolina. When Cathy's and Margaret's families both moved from the area, the girls were lonesome for each other. Cathy was extremely unhappy at the high school she attended at the time. She said there were too many gangs, the teachers didn't care about her, and she wasn't able to make friends. So she decided to go to New York to live with Margaret and her mother. Although Sue didn't like her leaving, she did not try to stop her. At this point in the story, Cathy stopped and wanted someone else to talk.

Sue then began with a little of her background. She stated that she had been born in North Carolina, where she and her brother were raised in an orphanage. Her mother had been institutionalized when the children were growing up. Sue had four half-sisters. Because she was looking to be a part of a family, she had moved back to North Carolina seven years ago. As a result of that move, she came to know her stepsisters.

Marcy spoke next. She recalled that she had remained behind with a second cousin Shannon when the family moved to North Carolina. (Later she revealed that Shannon was also her lover, which caused problems with Robert when Shannon moved into the family's apartment.) She said that she missed her family and was glad when they returned to the city. She also mentioned that she had dropped out of high school and had been working in a bank in the maintenance department. She intended to take typing classes so that she could get a better job.

The next person to speak was Dick. He related that when the family moved to North Carolina he had had a hard time adjusting to being in the South. He reported that he fell in with a gay crowd, where he felt more at home. He stated that he had recently worked at two different nightclubs. He became concerned about the drug and alcohol abuse among the employees, and so he alerted his boss to the problem, thinking that his boss would support him. However, his boss did not, and one night Dick and another employee walked off the job. He said that he was proud of quitting but not proud of walking off the job. He related that he wanted to experience many different types of jobs before deciding where he wanted to go.

The focus of the session then moved back to Cathy when Sue expressed her concern about how all the moves might be affecting her. According to the school counselor, Cathy had been having many up-and-down moods and periods of withdrawal. She also appeared to the other girls to be snobby. She had been referred to a local hospital for counseling, but Robert wanted to stop the counseling because of the expense. He felt that the $25 her father sent her each month should be used to pay for the therapy, but Sue would not hear of it. She believed that the adults in the family should pay for Cathy's counseling.

Cathy and Robert both acknowledged that they wanted to move to the suburbs and away from the chaos of the city. Cathy wanted a decent education and a school that had a dance program; Robert wanted a nice environment for all of them. He also felt that if he could get Dick and Marcy out of the city they might not be such night owls.

At this point the supervisors requested more information about the family's many moves. Sue was asked to fill in some of the gaps. She informed them that she was married from 1964 to 1975. However, there were many problems in the marriage, and in 1973 she separated from her husband. But six months later they decided to get together again and moved to southern Illinois, where they had lived before and where they felt more comfortable. But before actually settling in there, they went to Texas to visit Sue's father-in-law. They left Dick there for one month while they moved to southern Illinois.

By this time it was evident to the therapists that this family was constantly on the move and that these moves had greatly affected them. When this idea was presented to Sue, she said she felt the moves were her fault. She agreed that the moves had hurt the family a great deal. It was becoming clearer to the therapists that when Sue felt alone, trapped, or scared, she moved. When she was uncomfortable, as she seemed to be when discussing these moves, she giggled. A homework assignment was given to Sue to help her and the therapists understand all the moving. She was asked to draw a time line of her family, beginning with her first marriage.

As Sue continued with her story, she spoke of a new character, Jerry, who came to live with her and the children when they moved to North Carolina. He apparently had been in and out of Sue's life for about ten years. Sue related that Jerry picked on Dick then in the same way that Robert picked on him now. Sue stated that she was sick of all the conflicts. She said, "Dick is very special to me—all my kids are. I'm very protective of my kids." She acknowledged that she was tired of the conflict and feeling like she was always in the middle and that this feeling of being trapped in the middle made her want to "run" again to save herself and keep herself happy.

Sue asked Dick to say more about his relationship with Robert. Dick responded that he felt Robert was jealous of his relationship with his mother. Robert became sullen and refused to reply. It was then time to end the session. Since Sue had been given a homework assignment earlier in the session, the other family members were asked to write down what they felt needed to be improved in the family.

Sue and Cathy were the only family members who attended the second session. Sue was visibly upset. Dick and Robert had gotten into another argument just before coming to the session. Robert was angry that Dick didn't have to come because he was starting a new job. Therefore, Robert refused to come as well. Marcy didn't come because Sue had failed to remind her of the session. She claimed that she had no clean clothes and needed to do her laundry.

As the session began, Sue discussed her belief that Robert was jealous of her relationship with Dick. She stated that she wanted Robert to be less possessive of her so that she could help Dick. She didn't want to push her children away from home. "You can't replace your kids," she stated. When questioned about her homework assignment, she said that she had completed it but lost it and had not had time to do another one before the session.

Sue and Cathy both spoke freely of their frustration with Robert. They related that he bought them flowers, candy, and other gifts, some of which were expensive. Then he would tell them how much he had spent on them with the expectation that they would pay him back if he and Sue ever split up. That angered Sue a great deal. Instead of enjoying the gifts, she wondered how much they had cost. Sue saw some irony in Robert's behavior in that he worried and complained about the bills constantly and yet ran up the bills with his gift-giving. Sue also stated that she was embarrassed to go out with Robert because of his drinking. She refused to go out with her co-workers because Robert became loud and rude. She believed that his drinking was the reason that he had no friends. She said that she would rather stay home and rent a movie than be embarrassed by Robert. She reported that her friends had told her that Robert was too possessive of her free time and that she was losing her friends and possibly her kids. She viewed Robert's drinking as similar to her former friend Jerry's drinking in that Jerry became moody and irrational when he drank. Her husband had not been a drinker, but Sue stated that she felt somewhat smothered by him. As Sue continued with her story, she revealed that when she was unhappy and feeling trapped, she tended to flee. For example, she had not been happy in her marriage and so had fled to Jerry.

Cathy continued the discussion concerning Robert. She said that she basically got along with him when he was not drinking. She, too, felt hurt when he bought her something and then reminded her how much it had cost. Sue and Cathy agreed that Marcy also got angry with Robert, mainly because his constant swearing annoyed her. They reported that the swearing escalated when he was drinking. Sue also reiterated the fact that Dick and Robert were "always going at it" and that this occurred whether or not Robert had been drinking.

The focus of the session then switched to the different responsibilities of each family member. Sue admitted that she had trouble writing down the jobs of each family member and even more trouble with follow-through. So Marcy had taken it upon herself to write a list of the things that needed to be done and who should do them. But it worked only for a little while. Cathy felt she was too busy to do the jobs on the list because she worked long hours at the card shop—mainly to avoid the confusion at home. Marcy paid her rent, cleaned her room, and also cleaned the whole apartment when she could no longer stand the mess. Dick did little or nothing around the house. Robert usually cooked the main meal. No one seemed to be taking responsibility for cleaning up.

Sue then discussed her childhood. She related that she and her brother had been raised in an orphanage in North Carolina. Her mother had had a nervous breakdown, and Sue's father felt that he couldn't raise the children properly. Her mother eventually died of cancer when Sue was eleven. Sue had heard that her mother was wild, slept around, and was neglectful of her children. Sue was concerned that she would go crazy like her mother had done. She stated that she felt secure in the orphanage and enjoyed it. She was sad when she had to leave because her father remarried. His new wife was an alcoholic and was jealous of the relationship between her husband and his daughter. Sue and her brother lived with their stepmother for only one month when their father left his wife and moved to a city in the Midwest with the two children. There the three of them lived in a two-room apartment with their father's older daughter by a previous marriage. Sue remained in the city, where she met and married her husband. She once again mentioned that she had four half-sisters who were much older than she and that they all had the same mother.

The focus of the session then shifted back to the family's current situation. Cathy felt that Robert, rather than Sue, was the primary parent in the family. She also felt that Robert always overruled Sue and was, in fact, the one who set down the rules. Sue seemed to go along with Cathy's view. Cathy believed that the reason there was so much confusion in the family was because no one knew who the boss was.

## IV. INTEGRATIVE EVALUATION

**Structure:**


**Roles:**


**Communication/Perception:**


**Themes:**


**Individual Personality Dynamics:**

## V. FAMILY ASSESSMENT CARD

The assessment of your family's strengths and weaknesses is based on observation and clinical evaluation by your therapists in consultation with the supervisory staff.

The assessment will provide important information for your family. A commitment by each family member to work on mutually agreed-upon goals both in the sessions and at home between the sessions will maximize the value of this assessment. Work on each of the goals will help your family to function more effectively and help each family member to change and grow.

_____

_____

_____

_____

_____

_____

_____

_____

_____

_____

_____

_____

_____

_____

_____

## VI. COMPLETED INTEGRATIVE EVALUATION

**Structure:**
Rigid boundary and conflict in parental subunit; rigid boundary isolates Robert from the family; lack of a parental team; diffuse boundary between Sue and her children resulting in bad parenting

**Roles:**
*Expectations:* Inappropriate, nonmutual, unclear, inconsistent
*Consequences:* Inappropriate, inconsistent, unclear, nonmutual
*Follow-through:* Inconsistent, sporadic

**Communication/Perception:**
*Communication:* Overtalking by Sue and Robert; yelling by all family members; blame statements that lead to defensive reactions;
*Perception:* Lack of listening because of defensiveness and anger

**Themes:**
Lack of financial responsibility; Sue and Robert not an adult unit nor a parental team; alcohol abuse; irresponsible behavior; nonacceptance of Robert as a parental figure; nonacceptance of homosexual lifestyles

**Individual Personality Dynamics:**
*Sue:* Pattern of fleeing conflict; overprotective of children; use of avoidance and denial
*Robert:* Heavy drinker; inappropriate behavior; impulsive and irresponsible
*Cathy:* Fear of rejection; avoidance of conflict
*Dick:* Lacking an individual identity
*Marcy:* Emotional distancing

## VII. FAMILY ASSESSMENT CARD

> The assessment of your family's strengths and weaknesses is based on observation and clinical evaluation by your therapists in consultation with the supervisory staff.
>
> The assessment will provide important information for your family. A commitment by each family member to work on mutually agreed-upon goals both in the sessions and at home between the sessions will maximize the value of this assessment. Work on each of the goals will help your family to function more effectively and help each family member to change and grow.
>
> 1. Sue and Robert need to teach each other how to parent adult children together.
> 2. Sue needs to be aware of her tendency to avoid difficult situations (conflict), which then creates instability in relationships.
> 3. All need to work on listening and understanding what each family member is saying.
> 4. All family members need to understand that blaming creates defensiveness, which leads to fighting.
> 5. Responsibilities of each family member need to be clearly identified and understood.
> 6. Sue and Robert need to develop clear and consistent consequences for unacceptable behavior.

## VIII. ASSESSMENT SESSION (SESSION 3)

Sue, Cathy, and Marcy came to session three. Robert still refused to come because Dick wasn't coming. The therapists went over the assessment cards with those present. As they read over the cards, Cathy wanted to know if each card had the same thing on it or if each family member had different things they were to work on. It was explained to Cathy, Sue, and Marcy that the assessment cards were all the same so that the entire family knew what it needed to work on in order to function more effectively.

The therapists addressed the first goal. It was pointed out to Sue that she and Robert needed to work more as a parental unit. In that way, they could deal with Dick more effectively, thus relieving some of the tension between Robert and Dick. Sue said that she understood the goal and hoped that she and Robert could do it. When the second goal was discussed, Sue stated that she realized that she avoided conflict by fleeing and that this avoidance had created instability in relationships. She could see that happening between her and Robert. Marcy reacted positively to the discussion of the third goal. She saw Dick and Robert yelling first and listening second. She stated that she hated that style of communication. Loud conversations embarrassed her. Sue reported that Robert also yelled at her first and then later talked with her. This bothered her very much. She felt, however, that she did listen to and understand her children.

All family members agreed that the fourth feedback statement fit the family. Cathy related a story that illustrated the blaming and defensiveness. She had hidden $20 under Sue and Robert's mattress that previous weekend. When she went to get the money, it was gone. She blamed Robert, who became defensive, fought with Cathy over her accusation, and then proceeded to accuse other family members. Sue said that Robert always blamed family discord on Dick, who then became defensive and fought with Robert. Robert also yelled at Sue when he was really angry with Dick. That, in turn, made Sue frustrated and angry.

The fifth goal was discussed. Sue recognized that the house was often a mess, which led to yelling and blaming because chores had not been done. Marcy had made out a schedule of responsibilities, but it was rarely used or enforced. Marcy wanted Sue to make a duty chart, as she felt that the family really needed one. Cathy suggested that the family have a conference in the kitchen and make a list together. Sue and Marcy liked that idea and intended to pursue it.

The sixth goal was for Sue and Robert to develop and enforce clear and consistent consequences. Yelling and fighting were not acceptable, since consequences like that led nowhere. Sue stated that she avoided setting consequences because she was not able to enforce them consistently. The therapists encouraged Sue to work with Robert as a parental team in this area. Sue replied, ''Maybe I can do it with Robert's help.''

The session then moved on to the time line that Sue was to construct and then share with Cathy and Marcy. Sue had lost the first one and had hastily written a second one. She had not yet shared it with the girls. But she had asked them to write down major events from their own lives and to add them to the time line. They had not done this task and stated that they had forgotten it. Dick had refused to participate. As a result, the time line was vague and incomplete. It was missing important events, such as graduations, oldest daughter's wedding, significant men in Sue's life, and so on. Sue was asked what it had been like for her to compose the time line. She replied, "I felt bad. I left the kids' father and wasn't divorced and went to live with someone else. We moved a lot." She said that she had not realized how often she and the children moved until she wrote the time line.

At the end of the session homework was assigned. Robert and Sue were to list all the chores that they could think of that needed to be done around the apartment. They were also to think of consequences for chores not done. Then they were to call a family conference to see if other family members saw areas that needed more work. The girls were to develop their own time lines. All present seemed willing to do the tasks.

## IX. SUBSEQUENT SESSIONS

The following week the family did not show up or call to cancel. When the therapists called to see what had happened, Sue answered the phone. She said that she had started to come but had turned around and gone back home. She related that Robert still refused to attend and that the girls and Dick were working. While in the car she had become quite discouraged and decided that the therapists probably wouldn't want to see her alone. Sue was encouraged to come alone should this happen again. A fourth session was rescheduled for two weeks later.

Sue, Cathy, and Marcy arrived on time two weeks later. Robert still refused to attend. Sue stated that she thought that Robert might be rebelling by not coming, although she couldn't figure out why he might need to rebel. Cathy stated that she thought that it was important for Robert to attend, since he played a main role in the family. She stated, "Mom, you can't make him come, but you can be more assertive. Tell him that you prefer that he come." Marcy replied that she didn't care whether or not Dick and Robert came. Sue again mentioned how Robert's drinking embarrassed her. She said that she wished he was sober whenever he asked her to marry him. The therapists then questioned Sue about her feelings concerning Robert's drinking. She replied, "I don't want to be with a drunk. I get angry and hurt. I ignore him. I feel that he is possessive and jealous of me. I feel like he is suffocating me. He wants more love and attention than I can give. He always wants things his way." Marcy related that Robert had been so drunk and obnoxious the previous Friday night that she had retreated to her room to get away from him. She stated that she was disgusted with his behavior. The therapists asked Sue what it was that was keeping her in the relationship. She said that she didn't want to break her lease. She was asked what she was going to do if Robert continued to refuse to attend counseling. She replied that she would live with him for four more months until her lease was up in April and then move out.

The subject of Robert was then dropped and attention given to the time line Sue had done earlier. It was pointed out to Sue that there was no mention in the time line of Jerry, her former companion for ten years. Sue recognized that and the many other gaps in the time line. Cathy had completed her own time line but had forgotten to bring it. Marcy had not done the assignment. The therapists requested that Sue go over her time line with the girls. Then they were all to add items to Sue's line. The purpose of this intervention was to stop the avoidance behavior that had been going on.

As Sue was going over her time line with Cathy and Marcy, one of the therapists went to consult with the supervisor. It was agreed that Robert was a big part of the family's problems. In order to allow Sue, Cathy, and Marcy to express their feelings about him, it was decided to put an empty chair representing Robert in the middle of a circle and to have each family member tell "Robert" what they really thought and felt. Sue began. At first she laughed, but then she said, "Robert, I'm not especially happy with your drinking. I feel so unhappy that I want to do something about it. I'd be happy if you'd stop your drinking and come to counseling with us. If you don't stop drinking, I'll have to leave you. I get anxious that this is the same pattern I've had for ten years. I'd feel guilty about leaving you because you buy me things. But I get mad that you buy me things, because you then say that I have to pay you back. That disappoints and frustrates me. I feel like you're trying to buy my love. When we have fights, you then buy me flowers and dinner. I'd rather you stop doing the things that you do and just work on our relationship. I want you to talk to me about all sorts of things, not just your work. And I want you to listen to me. I have problems too. I'm angry and feel cornered and suffocated by you. I want to do something. I hate coming home because you're drunk. I'm humiliated when we get thrown out of places. What am I going to do with you?" With that last comment, Sue said she felt that she had said it all and was finished.

Then Cathy began. "Robert, you make our whole house miserable. You complain about Dick, and you're always talking about your problems at work. You're possessive of Mom, and Mom is unhappy. When Mom is unhappy, I'm unhappy. You have me confused. Are you two going to stay together just until April? I'm confused about that. I relate to you as my mother's boyfriend. I don't respect you because of your drinking. Besides, you put me down for my clothes. You won't take me out and pay for my dinner. I have to pay for it. You make me feel like a little kid.

I feel like getting really mad." Cathy's face was turning red. She said that she had nothing more to say.

Marcy was last. She stated, "I just can't talk to him. He only cares for Mom. He should love all of us." Marcy started to cry. Then she continued, "He just wants her. He wants Dick and me to move. If they get together, we're out of the family. I feel very hurt about that. Cathy's young and will go with them. I'm not ready to go out into the world yet. He brainwashes Mom to get rid of us."

Sue interrupted to say that she was not thrilled about the possibility that Dick and Marcy might move out. She said that she realized she had hurt and failed Marcy. She said to her, "I do want you in my life." Marcy replied, "I need the security of a home. I lived with Shannon and it was hard. There wasn't someone to lean on." At this point a perception check was initiated. Sue gave feedback to Marcy about what she had just said. Marcy responded that Sue had heard her correctly. Sue then went on to say that, if the tasks assigned to each family member were done, they probably could remain a family. The therapists pointed out that family chores had still not been worked out and that this was another way in which the family avoided conflict. Cathy stated that she wanted family rules set down so that there wouldn't be so much confusion. She felt that she could do better in school if the family were more organized.

Marcy then announced to the group, "Dick and I are gay. Shannon is my lover, but it's better not living with her. I want the family to work things out." Since the therapy session was almost over, there was not time to explore with Marcy what Robert's feelings might be about this issue.

Homework was then assigned. Since Robert and Dick were not participating in the counseling sessions, Sue and the girls decided to go to breakfast together on Saturday. At the breakfast meeting they would discuss some of the duties Sue had written and perhaps add more. On Sunday there would be a family meeting to determine who would do what and when. If someone did not attend, they would still be given tasks to do. Consequences would also be discussed at this meeting. The session ended with Sue and the girls looking forward to their Saturday and Sunday meetings.

Robert, Sue, and Cathy came to session five one week later. This session was difficult because Robert had been drinking. The therapists could smell alcohol in the room. Robert was obstinate during the first half of the session.

The planned weekend family meetings had not taken place. Many excuses were given. The therapists observed that this was a good example of how the family tended to avoid important issues. Robert loudly disagreed. He felt that it wasn't avoidance on his part but a matter of his having no control in the family. Sue stated that there had been more fights again about who would do the dishes and more yelling among family members in general. Robert admitted that he and Dick were not getting along and that they were always at each other. The therapists questioned the family about what had happened to the plans for family meetings. Sue, Marcy, and Cathy had attempted to write down the jobs that needed to be done for the family to function better. Robert was asked to join them but chose not to, as he wanted to set up his new stereo. Sue and the girls were so frustrated that they decided to proceed without him. No family meeting had been called for Sunday. Cathy said that she felt that the family should have met but that she had made plans to meet a friend. Sue said she felt helpless. She realized that she had failed to assert her parental authority.

Robert was then asked why he had come to the session. He replied, "I came to make Sue happy." Sue stated that she felt that he came just to make up for all the fighting that had been going on between them. "It's the same as if you bought me a teddy bear," she said. Sue and Robert both agreed that they had been fighting more and more. Robert asked Sue to explain why they were arguing so much, but the therapists asked Robert to state his views on the subject. He replied that it was because of money problems. "Sue wants to live on my money. She has more love for those kids than she does for me. I feel left out, and that makes me angry." Sue then asked Robert why he felt left out. Robert wanted Cathy to leave the room so that he could discuss the matter with Sue privately. Cathy responded, "I hate being around them when they're like this. They can't solve anything. I get so aggravated with them." Robert snapped to Cathy, "You're just as moody as I am." Sue added, "I miss the kids because they all fight when you're around." At this point Robert walked out of the session.

Sue reacted to Robert's leaving with frustration and anger. She said that she thought of leaving him whenever he acted like that. She added that he seemed childish and that he disappointed her. She related that she had written down her feelings on paper. Robert found the paper and ripped it up. She was hurt and frustrated and felt like she had no privacy. She again stated how torn she felt between Robert and her children and how she missed the children when they weren't around. But when they were all together, she said, there were always fights. Sue then discussed her relationship with Robert. "I'd like to talk to him without yelling and have him listen to me," she said. "If he's going to stay we have to work things out or March 31st it's bye-bye for me." Cathy replied that she was not sure Robert wanted to work things out.

At that point Robert returned to the room. There were only minutes left in the session. Sue asked him why he had left. He replied that he had gone to the bathroom. (He had actually been sitting in the waiting area.) Sue stated, "I want you to talk with me and listen to me and not yell all the time." Robert did not respond to Sue's statement. Instead he said that there would be less yelling if people would do the dishes. Cathy stated that she went to school, worked, and cleaned the house a little. She said she was so frustrated by the lack of order in the house that it made her not want to come home. It was agreed that everyone was frustrated by the lack of order. Therefore, another attempt at a family meeting to resolve this issue would take place on Sunday morning at 10:00. Robert and Sue would run the meeting. Sue would tell Marcy and Dick about the meeting so that they could make plans to attend. Robert left the session less agitated; Sue and Cathy were hopeful that the family meeting would, in fact, take place.

Robert and Sue attended the sixth session one week later. They related that the family had indeed met on Sunday as planned. It lasted three hours and covered thirteen areas of concern. The only problem at the meeting was that Marcy confronted Robert about his swearing. He then left the meeting because he feared that he might "lose his cool" with her. Eventually, however, he returned.

At the meeting the first issue discussed was communication. There were seven points under that subject. The family agreed that all seven points were important, but no consequences were set for not following communication guidelines. In fact, that seemed to be the problem with all thirteen areas—no clear consequences had been set down by Sue and Robert. Sue understood what the therapists meant by "no clear consequences." Robert, however, seemed ambivalent. He didn't feel that he and Sue could act as a parental team. He believed that the children would rebel against him. "Besides," he said, "Sue sticks up for the kids, especially Cathy. I put so much money into this family, and I can't say anything. These kids just don't want us to be happy."

At this point a "structure card," which graphically demonstrated family structure, was shown to Sue and Robert. The card showed the adult, parental, and sibling units with clear boundaries between each one. An example was given to help Robert understand the concept of an adult subunit. It was pointed out that he and Sue had failed to work out a clear budget. Both Sue and Robert then began to understand more fully the importance of having an adult subunit that was not invaded by the children. They also realized that they needed to work out their money concerns.

Robert then shifted the topic to the fact that Dick had not repaid the $70 he had borrowed. He also stated that he should be like a dad to Dick but that Dick wouldn't let him. Sue replied, "Leave Dick alone. You pick on Dick too much. You can't yell and nag at him, he doesn't listen." To the therapists she said, "I can't talk to Dick because Robert gets mad at me." They pointed out to her that what she had just said was a blame statement, as mentioned on #4 of the assessment card, and that blaming led to defensiveness, which led to fighting. Sue understood and agreed that she often did that where the children were concerned. She then accused Robert of leaving himself out of the family. The therapists asked her to explain how he did this. She said that he often walked out of the room or yelled rather than discussing with a person or the family what was bothering him. She gave as examples of this the previous therapy session and the family meeting. Robert agreed that he frequently did that and was able to see how this behavior removed him from the family.

Sue and Robert agreed to work on their adult and parental subunits. They would work on a budget together. They would also develop some clear and consistent consequences in the areas discussed at the family meeting, especially in the area of household chores.


## X. TERMINATION AND FOLLOW-UP

After a four-week holiday break, the family was contacted in order to schedule the next session. The therapists spoke with Robert and Sue, who told them that another session was not needed at this time. They felt that the family was getting along well together and that everyone was doing what they were supposed to do. The arguing and yelling had decreased, and home chores were being completed in a reasonable amount of time. Sue and Robert felt that they were beginning to manage their money better and were looking forward to their time together.

Despite the reported changes, the therapists encouraged the family to schedule a review session. They discussed the need to reinforce the positive direction of the family and to alert them to any unexpected pitfalls. Robert adamantly declined any further contact. Sue agreed with him but not as forcefully. The therapists inquired about Robert's drinking. Both replied that it was no longer an issue in their relationship. The therapists then suggested to the family that they could call for a future appointment when they felt that they were ready to continue in counseling. Robert and Sue agreed to do so and thanked the therapists for their time and service.

A follow-up call six months later was unsuccessful. The number was no longer in service. A call to the referring school counselor elicited more information. Cathy had left school three months earlier in the middle of spring term. She had returned to North Carolina with her mother so that they could be closer to other family members. She had planned to continue high school in the new location. Sue had left Robert, and his whereabouts were unknown. Dick and Marcy had remained in the metropolitan area and were thought to be living with friends.

# XI. THERAPIST REACTION AND EVALUATION

It was unfortunate that the Sommers family terminated abruptly and prematurely. However, this method of dealing with termination was characteristic of Sue's style of dealing with difficult situations. For over twenty years she had a history of brief relationships, frequent household moves, and abrupt job changes. She and her children were frequently separated by these moves, and so other caretakers were enlisted as needed. Sue could apparently tolerate only short periods of responsibility for her children and then needed to distance herself from them by relocating. Robert was but one in a long list of lovers and companions. His history of impulsivity, irresponsibility, and alcohol abuse made him a poor candidate to change Sue's patterns or to reunite and stabilize the family. Considering the unstable and chaotic family history, the children were reasonably responsible and able to care for themselves. As young adults, Dick and Marcy were self-supporting and had formed satisfactory peer relationships. They undoubtedly would need future assistance in goal setting and occupational adjustment, but they seemed receptive to counseling intervention. Cathy's plans to graduate from high school and continue her education showed initiative and responsibility.

Despite the premature termination and the therapists' anticipation of future difficulty, several positive changes could be seen in the family system. Sue had become more aware of her history of avoidance and the chaos that the many changes had produced in her life and with her children. Her conflictual relationship with Robert, as well as her increasing dissatisfaction with him, had been highlighted. Her new-found ability to set reasonable limits may well have led to the breakdown of their relationship. This could be seen as a positive outcome for her. As she began to set more consistent expectations for her children, more harmonious and satisfying relations were established among all four of them. All family members, with the exception of Robert, had become more aware of their blame statements and of the fact that blame statements produced defensiveness and conflict. At termination they were taking steps to minimize them. The result was a lowering of tension in the entire system.

The supervisors and therapists rated the success of this family at the 25% level. A minimal number (20%–40%) of the goals that had been established in the third session were achieved. Several more sessions, it was believed, would have reinforced those changes that were beginning to emerge and would have moved the family into the midrange of goal achievement.

*Rating*

X

---

| 1 | 2 | 3 | 4 | 5 |
|---|---|---|---|---|
| no goals attained 0% | few goals attained 25% | half of goals attained 50% | most goals attained 75% | all goals attained 100% |

**10**

# The Classic Triangle: Intact Family

RONALD MELMAN
LINDA SMITH

Therapists: Charlotte Katz
Janice McIntyre
Supervisor: William M. Walsh

## I. IDENTIFYING DATA

The Santini family includes Rico, fifty-three, his wife Ellen, fifty-one, and their four children - Susan, twenty-seven, Derrick, twenty-four, Eileen, twenty-one, and Cathy, nineteen. Derrick currently lives at home with his parents. The two youngest children are both away at school, and the oldest daughter is married and living geographically near her parents.

The Santinis appear to be a relatively successful middle-class family. They live in a comfortable suburban community. Both parents present themselves as caring and responsible people who are also successful in their chosen professions. Rico is an electrician; Ellen is a teacher. All of the children have been provided the opportunity to attend college. Susan and Derrick have already completed their undergraduate work, and the two youngest girls are currently attending college out of the state.

## II. INTRODUCTORY MATERIAL

Rico made the initial phone call to the clinic regarding his deep concern for his son's depressed condition. It was recommended that Derrick become involved in individual counseling. It was understood by Rico that both he and his wife and possibly the other siblings would also become involved in the counseling process at some point.

## III. INFORMATION GATHERING (SESSIONS 1 AND 2)

Derrick came alone to the first session, as expected. He presented as an intelligent, introverted, neatly groomed, good-looking young man. His general affect, however, was rather flat and dull. He did appear, however, to have a sense of humor, smiling on occasion. He was also able to make consistent eye contact with the therapists.

The session began with the explanation of how this meeting and subsequent meetings would be conducted. Derrick was informed that all session would be videotaped with his permission, which he gave.

Derrick then related some of the details of his life. He reported that he had been a philosophy major in college but that he currently worked for a veterinarian, a job he hated. He felt that it was meaningless and beneath his ability. He also disliked his boss because he tried to intimidate him and often put him down. Derrick felt that he was constantly being taken advantage of in that, whenever there was a crisis or emergency, the problem was immediately put on him.

Derrick also related that he had been in the Peace Corps and had been stationed in a remote part of India. He had loved being in the Peace Corps. However, after his initial training period was over, he had been asked to go off by himself to set up a new program. He reported that he panicked and subsequently resigned, a move that he now considered to be a big mistake.

He talked at length of his recent involvement with a girl for about six months. She had since left him, but it appeared that he had not yet resolved his feelings about this relationship.

Another concern for Derrick was his inability to establish a satisfactory relationship with his father. He felt that his father bossed him around and at times even tried to intimidate him. He viewed his father as talking at him rather than with him and never listening to him. He saw his relationship with his mother as good and felt that she listened to his concerns. However, Derrick stated emphatically that he must quickly make plans in his life in order to leave his family home.

At the end of the session Derrick was given three tasks for homework. He was to invite his parents to attend the next session. He was to think about and write down some long-term goals and expectations for himself. He was also to begin to express to his parents what he expected of them.

Derrick and his parents were present at the second session. Once again the structure of this and future sessions was explained. In addition to information about the videotaping and the homework assignments, the presentation of the assessment cards during the third session was explained. The therapists then solicited more information about the family so as to better understand the family dynamics.

Rico talked about depression in his family when he was growing up. He stated that his father had committed suicide when he was about fifteen. He therefore had to assume adult responsibilities in the household at an early age, and his mother and younger brother became very dependent on him. As Rico talked, the therapists felt that he had quite a bit of unresolved hostility toward his father. Rico mentioned that he saw a lot of his younger brother in his son. He admitted that he and Derrick needed a lot of work in improving their relationship. He also stated that he was more comfortable relating to his daughters, possibly because they gave him more attention and affection.

Ellen appeared to be resentful of what she described as a real mess in the family. She seemed generally negative about the prospect of the family's ever having a chance to function more effectively. Ellen reported that she saw her husband reacting to their son in the same way that he reacted to his younger brother. She stated that she dealt with the tension in the house by crying and by protecting Derrick. However, she also stated that she viewed her relationship with her husband as fine as long as Derrick was not present or discussed. She added, "During a crisis situation, Rico comes through like a trooper." She reported that she always panicked whenever the possibility arose that Derrick would be returning home.

Derrick's perspective was that his father's communication with him was not real, that they communicated as though they were strangers. He stated that their communication never involved feelings and was very superficial. He said that he was always nervous around his father and that he purposefully avoided him when at home. He also said that when his dad praised him, he felt that it wasn't sincere. However, he also stated,

"It's not right to dump on Dad." The therapists asked him about his homework assignment. Derrick replied that he had given the assignment some thought but that he believed it was only "candy coating."

At the conclusion of the session, a homework assignment was given to the family. They were all to think about and write down what each needed from the others. It was emphasized that it was particularly important for Rico and Ellen to state what they expected from Derrick while he was at home. They were also to practice better listening skills. Ellen and Derrick both reacted negatively to the assignment. Derrick blurted out that he hated his father. Ellen stated that there would be a lot of arguing and that it would all be a waste of time because nothing would ever change.

## IV. INTEGRATIVE EVALUATION

**Structure:**


**Roles:**


**Communication/Perception:**


**Themes:**


**Individual Personality Dynamics:**

## V. FAMILY ASSESSMENT CARD

The assessment of your family's strengths and weaknesses is based on observation and clinical evaluation by your therapists in consultation with the supervisory staff.

The assessment will provide important information for your family. A commitment by each family member to work on mutually agreed-upon goals both in the sessions and at home between the sessions will maximize the value of this assessment. Work on each of the goals will help your family to function more effectively and help each family member to change and grow.

_____

_____

_____

_____

_____

_____

_____

_____

_____

_____

_____

_____

_____

_____

# VI. COMPLETED INTEGRATIVE EVALUATION

**Structure:**
Ellen and Derrick aligned, which isolates Rico; weak and conflicted parental subunit; conflictual relationship between Rico and Derrick; presence of Derrick weakens the adult subunit of Ellen and Rico

**Roles:**
*Expectations:* Ellen and Rico unclear and conflicted about their expectations for Derrick; Derrick has no expectations for himself, therefore, no follow-through; Derrick has distorted view of Rico's expectations for him, Rico not able to verbalize those expectations
*Consequences:* Parental subunit totally unable to agree on consequences for Derrick
*Follow-Through:* No parental agreement in this area, either

**Communication/Perception:**
*Communication:* Ellen communicates by getting panicky, crying, or giving negative messages; Rico gives double messages, interrupts, overtalks, mistrusts; Derrick communicates by avoidance or by manipulation
*Perception:* Totally affected by distortions about one another

**Themes:**
Lack of strong parental and adult subunit; avoidance of issues; hopelessness; depression; communication without feelings

**Individual Personality Dynamics:**
*Rico:* Domineering, cognitive, mistrusting of others, rigid
*Ellen:* The placater, overly responsible for family functioning, fearful, avoids conflict, childlike.
*Derrick:* irresponsible, no goals for self, self-blaming, manipulative, low self-esteem, anger

## VII. COMPLETED FAMILY ASSESSMENT CARD

> The assessment of your family's strengths and weaknesses is based on observation and clinical evaluation by your therapists in consultation with the supervisory staff.
>
> The assessment will provide important information for your family. A commitment by each family member to work on mutually agreed-upon goals both in the sessions and at home between the sessions will maximize the value of this assessment. Work on each of the goals will help your family to function more effectively and help each family member to change and grow.
>
> 1. Ellen, Rico, and Derrick need to improve their communication by practicing clear, direct statements.
> 2. All need to improve their listening skills, especially through the use of perception checks.
> 3. Ellen and Rico need to communicate to Derrick their expectations for him while he is living at home.
> 4. Rico and Ellen need to strengthen their adult relationship by sharing activities together.
> 5. Derrick needs to establish goals and expectations for himself.

## VIII. ASSESSMENT SESSION (SESSION 3)

During the third session the assessment cards were presented to the family. It was explained that the cards contained the therapists' objective evaluation of how the family functioned and what was needed to improve that functioning. The therapists emphasized that it was important that family members give feedback to clarify specific points of discussion.

Family members' reactions to the cards differed quite a bit. Derrick stated that he felt that the future would just fall into place for him. He didn't buy into the assessment card, as he could not see the value of setting up expectations for self. Rico openly admitted that he understood his relationship with his son on an intellectual level but that he had difficulty dealing with it on an emotional level. He said that he realized that he needed to learn to like Derrick but that he didn't know how to do that. Ellen seemed quite defensive. She tended to hide behind her cup of coffee, saying, "What do you mean?" whenever comments were directed towards her.

## IX. SUBSEQUENT SESSIONS

During the next four sessions the focus was on several issues that were stressing the family. The adult subunit had been weakened by Derrick's return to the family home. Both parents expressed the fact that they enjoyed doing activities together and away from the rest of the family. Therefore, homework assignments were given for the couple to get out of the house and spend more time together.

It was also of concern to the therapists that Rico and Ellen be consistent in their responses to Derrick. Ellen was often overprotective of Derrick, while Rico was more demanding, expecting all of his children to be very responsible and productive.

Another area of concern was the alignment of Derrick and Ellen, which isolated Rico. A homework assignment given to Rico and Derrick to strengthen their alliance was for them to plan an activity together in which Ellen would not be involved. Furthermore, Ellen was asked not to attend the fifth session so that the father-son relationship could be improved. It was also requested of Ellen that she take a vacation in terms of interfering in the daily interactions between her husband and son.

Faulty communications between Ellen and Rico and between Rico and Derrick were also problematic. Many of the future homework assignments would be directed toward this area. It was felt that Derrick made many assumptions in his interactions with his father. He often stated that his father did not take him seriously and that he did not think that he was being treated like an adult. It was also felt that Rico was not direct or honest in his communications with his son. During some of the sessions the therapists directed Rico and Derrick to engage in a dialogue in order to practice better communication techniques. The therapists also introduced the idea of perception checks and modeled their use. They specifically requested that Rico and Derrick use this technique whenever any sign of anger appeared during their interactions. Subsequent homework assignments often included the daily use of perception checks.

During the fifth session Derrick mentioned that he realized that his father always put his family first, that he would wear rags in order for his children to be properly dressed. Derrick seemed confused as to how he could express his feelings of appreciation to his father, so the therapists helped him to do this within the session.

Another major theme dealt with was that of expectations within the family. Rico, Ellen, and Derrick were asked to write down at least three expectations that they had for one another. They were also asked to elaborate on these expectations within the sessions. Because the therapists were concerned that communication at home often involved distortions, they controlled the dialogue among the family members within the sessions, in order to keep them all on task. Derrick had distorted the idea that his father was a perfectionist, that he could not speak his mind around his father, and that his father was functioning on a much higher level that he. The therapists confronted him on these distortions by asking him how he had come to these conclusions about his father. Derrick's response was to become anxious and to avoid eye contact with the therapists. He finally stated, "Most of the time I don't know what I am saying. Maybe I'm mad at Dad because I'm not as together as he is." Derrick was also confronted on his distortion of himself as helpless. The therapists told him that all behavior was purposeful and that they wondered what purpose his view of himself as helpless was serving. Derrick was encouraged to see that making changes in his life would be much more productive than self-blaming.

In later sessions other areas of concern arose. Ellen, who had been asked not to attend for several sessions, was requested to rejoin the group. The therapists explained to the family that Derrick consistently expressed certain terms or messages that were guaranteed to trigger certain responses from the family. The therapists labeled these messages "hot buttons." Some examples of the hot buttons that Derrick used were self-blame statements and any mention of depression or suicide. All of these kinds of messages invariably invoked a response from the family system, so that the system constantly revolved around Derrick's moods. As Ellen stated, "When Derrick is up, we are all feeling good, and when he is down, we all react accordingly." At this point the therapists felt that the family's labeling of any kind of down mood as "depression" only made that particular hot button hotter. It was also perceived that family members' enmeshment with one another also kept the hot-button system in operation.

When Ellen returned to the sessions after her three-week absence from therapy, the therapists asked her if she had noticed any significant changes around the house. She stated that the tension level had been reduced and that the Thanksgiving holiday had gone well, perhaps because the two younger daughters were home from school. She also mentioned that she felt very resentful when Derrick pushed her hot buttons because "it sucks me into his pathology."

During session nine, the therapists concentrated on strengthening the adult subunit. There was still strain between Rico and Ellen, and Ellen reported that Rico continued to overtalk and to cut off Derrick during conversations. Also, both parents seemed to have different agendas for Derrick. Rico viewed him as underresponsible, stating that it bothered him to see a grown man with nothing to do. Ellen, on the other hand, was still the placater who jumped in to protect Derrick at every opportunity.

During session eleven the therapists noted for the first time that there was a physical connection between Rico and Ellen. During a difficult moment, Rico reached over to his wife and touched her hand for support.

Sessions twelve through fifteen were conducted with Rico and Ellen only, as Derrick had left town to work on a kibbutz in Israel. The therapists took advantage of this situation by working on the adult subunit, especially in terms of the communication patterns. It was pointed out to Ellen that she acted as the "switchboard" for the family and that it was an awesome burden for her to be responsible for all the family's communication. The therapists realized, however, that this switchboard position actually allowed Ellen to protect the children from Rico and Rico from the children by filtering negative information. The result was that Rico had become isolated from his own children. It was suggested to Ellen that she stop being the switchboard and allow Rico the opportunity to interact more directly with the children, thereby avoiding assumptions and distortions. It was hoped that Ellen would become more assertive and less avoiding in dealing with situations and that Rico would become less compulsive and rigid and more trustful of others' abilities to do things around the house.

It was also pointed out to Ellen that she was overly sensitive to Rico's words and actions. But she expressed great reservation about confronting her husband. "You want me to set Rico off. I'm not going to do that. When I see him getting ruffled, I back off." Ellen's reactions to Rico were another indication of how she played the role of family placater, a role she had perhaps learned in childhood.

Because Rico continued to overtalk and to ramble, the therapists made a concerted effort to have him become more direct in his communications. He related that he had become more open in expressing his feelings, feelings that had not been expressed for a long time. He also disclosed his fear that the therapy sessions could destroy his marriage. He admitted to continuing to be rather mistrustful that others in the family were capable of doing a task correctly. (Recently, he had asked his wife if he could check the manner in which she was keeping the records in the household checkbook!)

In session twelve the therapists asked Rico and Ellen to write down a list of their respective needs and to present their lists to one another. Ellen asked to be listened to, to be as important as Rico, to be able to talk to Rico without his becoming angry, and to not feel controlled by

Rico. Rico wanted Ellen to be less sensitive, to not overreact, and to not feel so responsible for the family. He also wanted to express more of his feelings, to be more responsible for what was going on in the family, and to have better communications.

In session fifteen the therapists and the supervisor attempted to graphically explain to Rico and Ellen the dynamics of their family system and how certain behaviors might be a hindrance to further productive growth in the family. At this point Ellen began to balk at the idea of continuing therapy. She stated that it was not working and that things would never change. The therapists pointed out that the following themes were occurring continuously in the family system:

1. When Derrick was not present, Ellen and Rico were able to form an alliance.
2. When Derrick was present, Ellen and Derrick formed an alliance that caused Rico to feel isolated.
3. Ellen continued to avoid conflict and confrontation, although her word choices were sometimes inflammatory, triggering a reaction in Rico.
4. When Ellen avoided conflict, she lessened the tension in the family system, but the long-term result was that the family members never addressed their problems.
5. Both parents shared the responsibility for the avoidance of family problems. Ellen lacked ability to confront, and Rico enabled her to continue to avoid.
6. Both of their respective family histories had a dramatic influence on the way in which their current family functioned.

At the conclusion of this session, Ellen and Rico were given the homework assignment of continuing to practice their communication techniques. Rico and Derrick were to correspond with one another and were to express their true feelings toward each other in their letters.

In the final four sessions (sixteen through nineteen) only Rico and Ellen were present, as Derrick was still in Israel.

Ellen stated that Derrick had communicated to them that he planned to return home the following month. She appeared to be almost paralyzed by fear, saying that she had not yet recovered from his last stay. The therapists pointed out to her that this might be an excellent opportunity to work on her avoidance issues, but Ellen was emphatic that this would not work and that it would be futile to even try. Although she continued to avoid the issues, the therapists attempted to structure the session so that she would not be able to defocus. In contrast to his wife, Rico was relatively calm about Derrick's return and tried to be supportive of Ellen. He felt that the past week had gone well for both of them and believed that there had been significant improvement in their relationship. He stated that he had written to his son expressing his emotions. Ellen commented that Rico had done his homework but that she thought that the therapists probably thought that she had not done hers. She said that she had not shared her feelings about Derrick's return with Rico but that "I usually take Rico's lead—if he is not upset, I don't get upset." Concerning Derrick she said, "I don't really ever see Derrick's being settled. He will continually search and search. I really don't see any real success for him." The therapists pointed out to her that this was another example of how she reacted negatively to her son when he pushed her hot buttons.

In session seventeen the issue of hot buttons was again explored, as was the issue of family enmeshment. Ellen stated that she still was not clear about what the term "hot button" really meant. The therapists viewed this statement as an example of the way in which Ellen attempted to avoid and defocus. The therapists used the illustration of Derrick's letters. They pointed out to Ellen that when Derrick's letters were upbeat, she was happy, but when they were sad, she became very down. Toward the end of the session, the therapists decided to use a relaxation exercise. Ellen became somewhat defensive and resistant to participating but ultimately did go along with the exercise.

Session eighteen would turn out to be the last session in which both Rico and Ellen were involved. The therapists continued to concentrate on developing a better alliance between them and to have them mutually agree on a specific course of action for Derrick's homecoming.

Derrick had sent another letter, and Ellen was questioning the sincerity of Rico's reaction to it. She stated that she felt he was not being honest or direct with her and that she doubted his feelings. The therapists observed that his was an example of their communication problem, in that Ellen was making as assumption about her husband's feelings without checking it out with him. It was also mentioned that Rico was repeating himself quite often and that perhaps this could be a clue to Ellen that he didn't feel listened to. A third aspect of the communication problem was highlighted in Ellen's statement that she could only go so far before Rico felt threatened. The observation was made that Ellen challenged Rico rather than communicating with him.

At the conclusion of this session Ellen stated that she would not return for the final meeting, because she didn't agree with her husband as to how to integrate Derrick back into the household. Rico had suggested that his son make a small contribution to the household as part of

his responsibilities while at home. Ellen had blown up over this suggestion, saying that it was unacceptable to her. During the session she
avoided any attempt to engage her and Rico in dialogue about this issue.
She subsequently disengaged herself from any further therapy.

## X. TERMINATION AND FOLLOW-UP

Since the clinic would be closing for five months, this was to be the final
session. The family had known of and accepted that situation for the past
two months. For this session Rico came alone. The therapists focused on
the apparent separate agendas that he and his wife had regarding Derrick.
The therapists had suggested in previous sessions that it was extremely
important that the parents come up with a mutually agreeable arrangement concerning their son. But to date, that had not happened. Therefore,
it was suggested to Rico that he continue to be aware of and to improve
his communication with Derrick. The last segment of the session was
spent reviewing the goals from the assessment card that had been given
to the family in session three. Rico stated that he felt that he had become
more patient, more open, and not as quick to respond. He also mentioned
that he now understood Derrick a little bit better and that he was more
attuned to family dynamics.

The Santini family was contacted by the supervisor six months after
the final session. It was anticipated that the family might want to reengage
in therapy at the clinic or that they might have arranged for counseling
elsewhere. The second hunch proved to be true. Rico told the supervisor
that he and Ellen had sought marriage counseling in their community approximately four months previously. They were attending on a bimonthly
basis and both felt that it was productive. Rico said that they had struggled for two months to improve their relationship by using the tools the
clinic therapists had provided. It was particularly difficult for them when
Derrick returned home. However, things became better again after he left
to attend graduate school in the East. Rico attributed their desire to seek
further counseling to the pleasant yet difficult family counseling at the
clinic. He felt that at the end of that experience, they were better able to
communicate with one another and that that improvement resulted in
their being able to reach a mutual decision to seek marriage counseling.
He also stated that they were planning to terminate counseling in one
month and that their relationship was more than satisfactory. Both were
still uncomfortable with their relationship with Derrick, but they did not
want to address it in counseling at that time. The conversation ended
with Rico's thanking the therapeutic team for their help and incitement.

"Without that initial work," Rico stated, "we would not have pursued further help."

## XI. THERAPIST REACTION AND EVALUATION

The greatest and most challenging obstacle to successful therapy for this family was the subtle manner in which Ellen attempted to control the flow of counseling. It appeared that she was very uncomfortable and defensive with the process. She always seemed to be looking for an excuse not to attend the sessions. Much of the therapists' preparation for each session was spent in trying to determine ways in which Ellen might be more positively engaged in the therapeutic process.

Both therapists felt that Rico had made significant progress, that he had worked on the issues diligently, and that he had been quite sincere in his efforts.

It was never clear as to what Derrick's real agenda had been. The therapists were never sure where he wanted to go, as he appeared somewhat confused. He seemed to be aware of the manner in which he used the "hot button" issues to get his parents to react. The therapists regretted that they did not have the opportunity to explore with him his difficulty in staying with a project to its conclusion.

At the end of nineteen sessions there were still many unresolved issues. However, both therapists felt that many issues had been brought into focus for the family and that perhaps these issues would continue to be explored and resolved in future counseling.

*Rating*

|  |  | X |  |  |
| --- | --- | --- | --- | --- |
| *1* | *2* | *3* | *4* | *5* |
| no goals attained 0% | few goals attained 25% | half of goals attained 50% | most goals attained 75% | all goals attained 100% |